The Debater's Guide

Jon M. Ericson, James J. Murphy, and
Raymond Bud Zeuschner

The Debater's Guide

Third Edition

Southern Illinois University Press

CARBONDALE

Library of Congress Cataloging-in-Publication Data
    Ericson, Jon M.
    The debater's guide / Jon M. Ericson, James J. Murphy, and
    Raymond Bud Zeuschner.— 3rd ed.
    p. cm.
  1. Debates and debating. I. Murphy, James Jerome. II. Zeuscher,
Raymond F. III. Title.
PN4181.E65 2003   808.53—dc21
ISBN 0-8093-2538-1 (pbk. : alk. paper)   2003001748

Printed on recycled paper. ♻

The paper used in this publication meets the minimum
requirements of American National Standard for Information
Sciences—Permanence of Paper for Printed Library Materials,
ANSI Z39.48-1992. ⊛

To Don, Barrie, Edie, Mike,
Dan, Bob, Denise, Lynette, Rich, Chris,
Robin, . . . and all student debaters
learning to think critically
and to articulate clearly.

There are only two parts to a speech:
You make a statement and you prove it.
—Aristotle, *Rhetoric*

Contents

The Debater's Guide

The Value of Debate

I

Debate is one of the oldest activities of civilization. Calm, orderly debate, in which speakers argue for acceptance of various answers to a given question, is an obvious feature of modern parliaments and congresses. But it also had its place even in the deliberations of ancient kings, who maintained councils of nobles to give them advice. When the nobles disagreed, they were allowed to debate their proposals before the king, who acted as the final judge in choosing one plan of action.

In modern democratic societies, the right to debate is a priceless asset. It enables any citizen to propose a better plan of action than the one that the ruling power sets forth. If the speaker can convince enough citizens that the new idea is a better one, then the speaker can change the policy of the city, county, state, or even nation.

In the United States, there are various ways in which the effective speaker can propose a new solution to a problem. One way, for instance, is to persuade a number of people to sign a petition to put a proposal on the ballot in an election. Then the proponents can speak to the voters on behalf of the proposal and perhaps convince a sufficient number of them of the need to vote it into law. They will undoubtedly meet outspoken opposition if they attempt to use this method of expressing their opinions, and it is essential that they know what to do in this kind of debating situation. By the same token, a good speaker can defend the present system, or status quo, by opposing unsound ideas. We are accustomed to the formal debating done by members of legislative bodies such as the Senate or the House of Representatives. In these houses, elaborate guidelines are laid out to ensure adherence to the two basic rules of debate: (1) present one issue at a time, and (2) provide equal opportunity for presentation of each viewpoint.

The committee system in the U.S. Congress, for example, makes it possible to begin debate on a bill even before it reaches the floor. But whether it is debated in a committee hearing (with the committee as judges) or on the floor of one of the two houses, the same basic principles are involved.

You may not be particularly conscious of the fact that debate occurs in every walk of life, not only in congresses. Actually, every situation in which you are asked to compare alternatives is one that forces you to debate the merits of those alternatives. Sometimes you will do the debating within yourself, as when you must decide whether to attend college. Sometimes the debating is done in your presence by others, with you as the judge, as in the case of rival sales presentations, each of which asks you to buy their particular product. Often we fail to recognize the debate situation because only one person is speaking to us—the single salesperson in a store, for instance—but usually that person reveals the true nature of the debate by acting as if there were actually a third person present with you. Such phrases as "You may be thinking that this would be expensive, but . . . " are signs of an awareness on the sellers' part that they must refute arguments that can be brought against their proposal by one part of your "self" so that the judge part of your self will decide in their favor.

Therefore the debating you do now can be a great help to you all your life. And you don't have to be a lawyer or member of Congress to use debating skills.

The Advantages for You

Since the first formal intercollegiate debate in the United States (between Harvard and Yale in 1892), hundreds of thousands, perhaps even millions, of American high school and college students have participated in academic debate. Woodrow Wilson engaged in debating as a student at Princeton long before he became president of that university, governor of his state, and finally president of the United States. Presidents Kennedy, Johnson, Nixon, Carter, and Clinton are recent examples of national figures who participated in debating during student days. But you can spend four or even eight school years in debating and come out with little benefit unless you know what it is you are trying to do and what it is you are trying to learn. *The Debater's Guide* is dedicated to two closely related ideas: first, that you cannot do a job well unless you know what the job is and, second, that you can never fully understand the job unless you are able to do it well. Therefore, you will find, the advantages of debate for you coincide exactly with the virtues of an ideal debater:

1. The ability to collect and organize ideas. A successful debate speaker is one who can absorb vast amounts of material and select from it those items that are the best to use in a particular debate.

2. The ability to subordinate ideas. A debater will hear about forty-five hundred to five thousand words from the opponents during a typical single round of debate. Together with a colleague, this debater will deliver an additional forty-five hundred to five thousand words. Only by sorting out the major ideas from the minor ones can any speaker hope to make sense of this flood of words.

3. The ability to evaluate evidence. Skill in gleaning the most important evidence is a hallmark of an intelligent speaker. Not every statement, quotation, statistic, or idea in a debate is worth the trouble of refutation.

4. The ability to see logical connections. Aristotle once pointed out that the ability to see what is similar among dissimilar things is a mark of genius. The great mass of data presented during most debates causes confusion among the hearers; therefore the speakers who can identify the relationship between items help to clarify the debate for the audience and thus improve their own chances of success.

5. The ability to think and speak in outline terms. Clarity is essential in a debate (and in any good communication, for that matter), during which the clash of ideas often confuses an audience. The debaters must have not only a perfectly clear mental outline of their entire case but also the ability to communicate the sense of that outline to the audience.

6. The ability to speak convincingly. An awareness of what an audience expects—what it takes to convince that particular

audience—is absolutely essential, both in debate and in other types of speaking.

7. The ability to adapt. Since a debate is a fluid situation, constantly changing as new ideas are introduced by various speakers, it places a premium on readiness of reply. In practice, this readiness means that you must be not only well organized, logical, analytic, and convincing but also able to react to new ideas quickly.

These are the skills that *The Debater's Guide* will make easier for you to develop. They will be valuable to you not only in your school debating but in every choice you make your whole life long, because every genuine choice involves a genuine debate.

In a larger context, that of the democratic society in which you live, your ability to present your point of view may be even more important, both to your own interest and to the interests of preserving and protecting that democratic society. As Adlai Stevenson has said, in "The Educated Citizen,"

> I would remind you of an axiom in political science: people get the kind of government they deserve. Your public servants serve you right. Our American government may be defined, perhaps, as the government that really cares about the people. Just so, our government demands, it depends upon the care and devotion of the people. (*What I Think,* ed. R. Keith Kane, 1956)

Debate skill cannot by itself make good citizens, but the American who cannot speak effectively in an organized way is a voiceless citizen, one whose good ideas may be lost in the crowd or are never heard. Debating, consequently, can be highly valuable both to you and to your society.

Understanding the Process

2

The Proposition

Almost every topic for school debate is a proposition of value or a proposition of policy. That is, it is a statement that asserts the value or worth of something or that some course of action should be followed—some new policy should be adopted. For instance, here are some school debate topics of past years.

Value-Oriented Propositions

RESOLVED: That education has failed its mission in the United States.

RESOLVED: That affirmative action promotes deleterious hiring practices.

RESOLVED: That a U.S. foreign policy significantly directed toward the furtherance of human rights is desirable.

RESOLVED: That the individual rights of privacy are more important than any other constitutional right.

RESOLVED: That the United States is justified in aiding undemocratic governments.

Policy Propositions

RESOLVED: That all U.S. military intervention into the internal affairs of any foreign nation or nations in the Western Hemisphere should be prohibited.

RESOLVED: That the federal government should significantly curtail the powers of labor unions in the United States.

RESOLVED: That the United States should significantly increase its foreign military commitments.

RESOLVED: That the federal government should significantly strengthen the regulation of mass media communication in the United States.

Speakers who wish to debate must first understand what they are trying to do when they agree to defend or oppose one of these statements. What is a value-oriented proposition? What is a policy proposition? What happens in a debate? We can best begin with a look at three types of topics: facts, values, and policy.

The Proposition of Fact: Describing the Present or the Past

Fact propositions are a form of debate question rarely used in school debating. An example might be "The cause of the midair collision was a faulty radio receiver" or "The defendant is guilty of murder." The proposition of fact asks for proof of the previous existence of a fact. It is always marked by what is called a linking verb—a verb like *is* or *was*. The only matter to be settled is whether a thing or state already exists. Consequently the proposition of fact always deals with the past: what caused a collision that has already occurred; who killed a person already dead? Even a proposition like "The Empire State building is 831 feet tall" deals with a past fact, since the building must exist prior to the statement. This time element is extremely important, because it limits such a debate to a yes-or-no reply. Because of this limitation, propositions of fact are seldom used for interschool debate, although they are almost exclusively the type found in the courtroom. They impose severe restrictions on the amount of evidence that can be gathered, as well as on the proposal of alternative solutions.

The Proposition of Value: Making a Judgment

In value-oriented topics, three elements are found.

1. The item being evaluated or about which the value judgment or judgments are being made. Usually, this item is the subject of the sentence, as in "Resolved: That free trade is desirable."

2. The verb, which tells whether the topic deals with a historical evaluation in the past tense ("Gen. Custer was unjustified in his battle strategy"), with a generalized statement ("Freedom of speech is the most important constitutional right"), or with future speculation ("Offshore oil development will be harmful"). In school debate, the generalized present tense *is* has been the most common verb.

3. The term doing the evaluation—for example, *harmful* or
   beneficial or *deleterious*.

The difficulty involved in this type of proposition is finding acceptable proofs for assertions that may seem subjective in nature. Criteria must be established by the affirmative side in the debate that apply to the evaluation. For example, what constitutes "desirable?" When do we reach the level of positive associations so that we move into the area called desirable? Thus the debate is often in two major parts: (1) the quality or reasonableness of the evaluating term and (2) the application of that term to the subject term of the sentence. Additional areas of case development, as well as refinements of these two elements, are in chapter 4.

The Proposition of Policy: Urging Future Action

In policy propositions, each topic contains certain key elements, although they have slightly different functions from the comparable elements of value-oriented propositions.

1. An agent to do the acting—"The United States" in "The
   United States should adopt a policy of free trade." Like the
   object of evaluation in a proposition of value, the agent is
   usually the subject of the sentence.
2. The verb *should*—the first part of a verb phrase that urges
   an action.
3. An action verb to follow *should* in the *should*-verb combination. For example, *should adopt* here means to put a program
   or policy into action through governmental means.
4. A specification of directions or a limitation of the action
   desired. The phrase *free trade,* for example, gives direction
   and limits to the topic, which would, for example, eliminate
   consideration of increasing tariffs, discussing diplomatic recognition, or discussing interstate commerce.

Propositions of policy deal with future action. Nothing has yet occurred. The entire debate is about whether something ought to occur. What you agree to do, then, when you accept the *affirmative side* in such a debate is to offer sufficient and compelling reasons for an audience to perform the future action that you propose.

When you agree to accept the *negative side,* you actually enter into a contract to offer sufficient reasons for an audience to reject the affirmative's arguments.

Ground Rules for American Debating

It should be clear at this point that the very nature of the debate encounter leads to certain ground rules, or general principles. The first of these principles is that one debate side agrees to attempt one kind of thing and that the other side attempts to counter that effort. More will be said about that agreement in a later chapter, but before leaving the matter of the debate proposition, it might be useful to look briefly at a further aspect of the debate itself.

When you agree to defend one approach to the debate proposition—whether the negative (*opposition* in British parlance) or affirmative *(government)* side—you also obligate yourself, in American debate practice, to limit yourself for that one debate to that single approach required by the terms of the debate. In other words, you agree to act as an advocate of only one point of view. This practice is contrary to British school debating, for example, in which a speaker usually can choose any point of view, can adapt that viewpoint to other speakers' sides as the debate progresses, and can even reverse argument and join forces with the opposition if desired. A debate topic in the Oxford Union and in many parliamentary-format tournaments in the United States is often phrased as a question or as a general expression of attitude: "Resolved, that this House deplores the Palestinian situation" or "Is there a solution to the Arab-Israeli crisis?" Many sides will thus be possible in such a debate format.

American debating involves matching two sets of advocates who have agreed to maintain consistently opposed viewpoints. This maintenance of side is true for American parliamentary style as well, even if the topic is phrased in the British format. This system is followed, literally, for the sake of argument. Such a contract with the opposing speakers and with the audience is entered into so that both affirmative and negative arguments may receive the undivided attention of one pair of debaters. From the standpoint of the audience, this procedure makes for efficiency of discussion—each side trying to present every available bit of evidence and reasoning in the best possible light. Each speaker benefits in two ways: first, by giving undivided attention to one approach to the problem and, second, by being required to reply to another speaker or speakers who have given equal thought to their specific approach.

Procedure
Sequence of Speeches

The standard American procedure usually calls for two persons to form a team and debate both affirmative-government and negative-opposition sides during a tournament. In the following examples, the term *affirmative* also means the "government" speaker in parliamentary style. Likewise, throughout this book, *negative* will also mean "opposition." The affirmative begins the debate by presenting a speech (the first affirmative, or prime minister, constructive) that makes a case for adopting the resolution. The next speaker is the first negative, or leader of the opposition, who is followed by the second affirmative (member of government) and, finally, the second negative (member of the opposition). Most tournaments also include cross-examination periods between each constructive speech. Without the cross-examination, the format is often termed *Oxford debate*. With the cross-examination periods, it is simply termed *cross-examination debate* or, sometimes, *Oregon style*. Parliamentary style usually features a form of cross-examination as part of the constructive presentations during which opponents may interrupt the person speaking with *point of information, point of order,* or *point of personal privilege* comments. There is usually no specific time set aside just for that purpose.

After a short pause, often omitted, the second negative constructive speaker is followed by the first negative rebuttal speaker. The speakers then continue to alternate again, with first affirmative rebuttal, second negative rebuttal, and finally, second affirmative rebuttal. Including cross-examinations, the sequence in most team debates is as follows.

Constructive Speeches
First Affirmative
    Cross-Examination by Second Negative
First Negative

Cross-Examination by First Affirmative
Second Affirmative
Cross-Examination by First Negative
Second Negative
Cross-Examination by Second Affirmative

Rebuttal Speeches
First Negative
First Affirmative
Second Negative
Second Affirmative

In parliamentary format, a common order is
Prime Minister Constructive (PMC)
Leader of Opposition Constructive (LOC)
Member of Government Constructive (MGC)
Member of Opposition Constructive (MOC)
Leader of Opposition Rebuttal (LOR)
Prime Minister Rebuttal (PMR)

The negative side has the last speech in the constructive series, while the affirmative has the last speech in the rebuttal series. This sequence equalizes the opportunity of reply, since the last speaker in a series has an advantage in this respect.

Time Limits

American high schools and colleges usually allow eight minutes for constructive speeches, three minutes for cross-examinations, and four minutes for rebuttals. In Oxford debate, high schools usually keep the 8-4 format, while colleges shift often to a longer 10-5 format. It is not unusual to find college cross-examination formats that are 8-3-5 or 10-3-5. Most time limits are a matter of custom and may be set by the host of a tournament or by association rules. There are also formats for one-person teams (called *Lincoln-Douglas style*) that vary in their time allotments. Parliamentary style frequently uses the following format.

PMC—seven minutes
LOC—eight minutes
MGC—eight minutes
MOC—eight minutes

LOR—four minutes

PMR—five minutes

In most parliamentary formats, speakers may be interrupted by opponents for questions or parliamentary inquiries during the speech. No matter which time format is selected, each side will have the same amount of time to present constructive arguments, to question the other team (if the format allows for it), and to respond in rebuttals.

The "Clash" Process
Making Every Moment Count

Within this time framework, the affirmative tries to compel the audience to agree that the resolution should be adopted. Support for the resolution means that the audience either accepts the affirmative team's judgments on a value-oriented topic or agrees that the future action suggested by the policy topic should be taken. The negative attempts to prevent the affirmative from succeeding. Since time is limited in a debate, it is true that every moment counts. Time is precious to the speaker. No time can be wasted. If you waste a minute aimlessly repeating yourself, it is a minute that can never be made up in that debate. If your opponent has spent one minute introducing three items of evidence or lines of reasoning against your case, you have lost out twice.

Moreover, a debate can be extremely confusing to an audience. Any human being who listens for forty-eight or sixty minutes to four other people arguing is probably going to be swamped by conflicting ideas. To the listener, there is too much time in a debate—that is, so many things are said during the debate that the listener finds it extremely difficult to keep track of what is going on.

Thinking and Speaking in Outline Terms

For these two reasons—the speaker's need for time and the audience's saturation with it—it is imperative that every debate speaker know exactly what to try to do at every instant of the debate. This awareness of what is going on must also be communicated to the listeners as well. Therefore, the first principle of successful debate speaking is to *think and speak in outline terms.*

In other words, debate speakers must know the main ideas in the debate. If they do not know their own main arguments, it is certain they will never be able to recognize those of the opposition.

The easiest way to visualize this principle in practice is to see the entire debate as two outlines set alongside each other. To think in outline terms is to view the debate case in its functional parts: issues, arguments, and evidence. For instance, in a debate on a particular policy proposition, the affirmative might outline part of their case as follows.

ISSUE: I. The present system of state and federal highways is inadequate, for

ARGUMENT: A. U.S. highways are substandard for present needs, for

EVIDENCE: 1. Specific supporting evidence.
                2. Specific supporting evidence.
                3. Specific supporting evidence.

ARGUMENT: B. Expansion under the present system is not adequate for future needs, because

EVIDENCE: 1. Specific supporting evidence.
                2. Specific supporting evidence.
                3. Specific supporting evidence.
                4. Specific supporting evidence.

ARGUMENT: C. Present federal help is inadequate, for

EVIDENCE: 1. Specific supporting evidence.
                2. Specific supporting evidence.

ARGUMENT: D. Present highways programs do not provide work projects to alleviate unemployment, because

EVIDENCE: 1. Specific supporting evidence.
                2. Specific supporting evidence.
                3. Specific supporting evidence.

If the audience heard only this speech, well delivered and with the use of adequate evidence (sufficient and compelling), they would be expected to agree with the speaker. Such a speech would contain what is called a *prima facie case*—that is, "on its face" or "at first look," it appears compelling. Likewise, a speaker presenting a well-organized and -supported first affirmative on a value-oriented topic that presents sufficient and compelling reasons to believe the value judgment would also have presented a prima facie case for the adoption of the resolution.

The Prima Facie Case and the Debate Clash

Debaters use the term *case* to mean all the assembled proof available for demonstrating the truth of the proposition (for the affirmative) or the untruth of the proposition (for the negative). A complete outline of a case is called a *brief.*

The Prima Facie Case

The affirmative must present a prima facie case—a collection of assertions and proofs sufficient to create belief in the proposition. This obligation is true for fact, value, and policy propositions. Suppose that no negative speaker were to appear; would it still be possible that when the first affirmative finished speaking, the audience would remain unconvinced? Speakers can lose by default if they fail to create belief in what they say. Technically, in a debate, *prima facie* refers to a case that establishes such a high degree of probability that the proposition must be accepted unless refuted. Thus, the clash is set up for us—the affirmative must offer a reasonably compelling case, and the negative is obligated to respond with refutation.

Establishing the Clash Areas

In a debate, of course, there is an opposing team of speakers. How should the first negative speaker reply? For the sake of clarity, the negative must also visualize their speeches in outline form. When the first negative finishes speaking, then, the audience might have the following opposing sets of outlines to consider.

Affirmative	*Negative*
1. The present system of state and federal highways is inadequate for four reasons.	1. The affirmative has said there are four deficiencies in the present system. We shall now review each reason from the negative perspective.

A. U.S. highways are sub-standard for present needs, for
  1. Evidence
  2. Evidence
  3. Evidence
B. Expansion under the present system is not adequate for future needs, for
  1. Evidence
  2. Evidence
  3. Evidence
  4. Evidence
C. Present federal help is not adequate.
  1. Evidence
  2. Evidence

D. Present highway programs do not provide work projects to alleviate unemployment.
  1. Evidence
  2. Evidence
  3. Evidence

A. American highways are the best in the world.
  1. Evidence
  2. Evidence
B. Expansion is suited to future needs.
  1. Evidence
  2. Evidence
  3. Evidence
  4. Evidence
  5. Evidence
C. Federal help is adequate.
  1. Evidence
  2. Evidence
  3. Evidence
D. Unemployment is not a real issue, for

  1. Evidence

If this pattern has been followed, two things have happened in the debate.

1. The speakers have shown the audience the opposing arguments and therefore have asked the audience to make a decision on the basis of evidence. The "clash" between ideas has been set up. It is now up to each side to show, on the basis of proofs, why its own conclusions should be accepted.

2. The negative speaker has declared that the negative team will not discuss the question of unemployment as a major idea. This decision narrows the debate to its essential points and heightens the clash between the two teams. The speaker has defined by exclusion the area of clash between the two teams.

Budgeting Time in the Clash Process

If the speakers realize that they must constantly be aware of their own arguments and those of the opponents, they will soon decide that they must not overlook any major ideas that might persuade their audience.

They face two difficult tasks. First, they must have a clear idea of what they wish the audience to accept. Second, they must speak in such a way that the audience never becomes confused. The first affirmative speaker has little to worry about in this respect because no other speaker has yet appeared to confuse the issues. The first affirmative also has the advantage of careful preparation and rehearsal of the speech so that each idea can be expressed exactly as planned. But each of the following speakers has a problem. By the time the last rebuttal presenter stands up to speak, for example, seven previous speeches, perhaps eight or nine thousand words in all, have been delivered. Add to that the four cross-examination periods with their questions and answers and the possibilities for confusion are obvious.

Therefore all debate speakers must speak in terms of a double outline—the outline of their own case and the outline of their opponents' case. As a consequence, they budget their time so that they are able at every major point to tell the audience what is going on. And they cannot thus enlighten the audience unless they have decided in their own minds exactly how much attention each idea is worth. Some sort of overall time plan is necessary.

Since each of the four speakers in a team debate faces a slightly different problem, each one has a different time budget. The following chart shows a normal time-budgeting plan based on the time limits used in typical high school and college debates.

Speakers' Duties

The approximate minimal duties of the various speakers in their constructive and rebuttal speeches are outlined below. These duties are suggestions for speech plans, and they provide a fairly useful and typical guide for debate speakers, whether just beginners or advanced champions; whether in team debate, Lincoln-Douglas contests, or parliamentary tournaments. Once a speech plan is chosen by the team, it should be followed as closely as possible. Avoid wasting time during the debate by attempting to create new duties or major modifications under the pressure of the time clock. The times suggested indicate both a job that needs to be done during the speech and a maximal allotment to that job.

Constructive Speeches

First Affirmative	Time (min.)	First Negative	Time (min.)
1. Define terms and criteria.	1	1. Refute (last chance on definition).	2
2. Outline (preview) entire case, including partner's.	.5	2. Outline (preview) entire negative case.	.5
3. Develop main case.	6	3. Develop main case.	5
4. Summarize.	.5	4. Summarize.	.5
	8		8

Second Affirmative		Second Negative	
1. Respond to challenge on terms and criteria.	2	1. Outline affirmative, refuting main points.	2
2. Repeat outline of affirmative case and refute negative case points, showing points negative ignored or failed to refute.	2	2. Repeat negative case outline, showing conflict with affirmative case, and indicating points unrefuted by affirmative.	2
3. Extend and reestablish affirmative case.	3.5	3. Extend and reestablish negative case.	3.5
4. Summarize case.	.5	4. Summarize case.	.5
	8		8

Rebuttals

Each rebuttal speech follows the same plan, whether the speaker is affirmative or negative. The two speakers on a side must split the outline between them, as in preparing a constructive case.

First Rebuttal

1. Identify the arguments of the opponents' entire case and list which ones each partner will take.   .5 min.
2. Refute those arguments selected as your responsibility.   3 min.
3. Summarize your team case.   .5 min.

Second Rebuttal (except in parliamentary or Lincoln-Douglas formats)

1. Follow the plan outline for the second negative constructive speaker, covering the remaining major arguments in three and a half minutes, saving at least thirty seconds for summary of the entire case and comparison with that of the opponents.

Understanding the Debate Process

If the speakers understand what they are trying to do at every stage of the debate and clarify the natural clash of ideas for the audience, the audience can then devote its attention to making an intelligent judgment based on the reasoning and evidence that each side brings forth. The whole purpose of public debate, as noted earlier, is to provide an opportunity for a rational consideration of alternatives. If the speakers confuse themselves and the audience, the entire effort at debate is a waste of time. To avoid such confusion, it is therefore essential that the debaters understand what they are trying to do. It is also essential that they budget their time, think in outline terms, identify the main issues, and cast aside the minor ones. Above all, they must keep the audience reminded of what is going on. We call this obligation the burden of communication, and all speakers carry it.

If speakers understand the debate process itself, they are then able to think more intelligently about the problem of proof, that is, to consider how they can persuade an audience to accept a statement they make. Even if that audience is a single judge in a classroom during a tournament, acceptance of argument is still the goal. The debate structure is the skeleton of the arguments; the proofs are its muscle.

This section has introduced you to some of the basic concepts and vocabulary associated with scholastic debate. Some of the initial concerns have been brought out, and some of the formats, propositions, duties, and times have been discussed. Review this introduction now so that you'll be ready to move to the next step of learning how to build a debate case.

Case Building: Underlying Concepts 3

More than two thousand years ago, Aristotle identified the debater's basic problem: "There are only two parts to a speech: You make a statement and you prove it." In modern debating, the two teams make a statement, in effect, when they agree to uphold either the affirmative or the negative side. The whole debating structure—the sequence of speeches, four on each side—is designed to make sure that each speaker has an equal chance to make a statement and to prove it.

When the debate process itself has been understood, then the basic questions to be answered are "What is proof?" and "How is proof used in a debate?"

The Problems of Proof
Creating Belief

It is obvious that merely stating a proposition will not make listeners accept it. If you say, "We should spend more for highway construction," all you have done is to assert that such a step should be taken. From the audience's point of view, you have merely raised the question "Why should we?" No person in that audience has any reason to believe that the proposal is good merely because you have voiced it.

If, however, you are able to say "Because . . . " and then list several reasons why each of your listeners should honestly make the same statement, you are likely to succeed in proving your point. You have succeeded when it is possible for your audience to make the same assertion that you do: when every audience member, if asked, would say, "Yes, we should spend more money for highway construction."

This apparently simple relationship—that is, the agreement

between speaker and audience—is the key to the whole problem of debate. If you can create belief in your statements, you can secure this agreement. *Proof,* therefore, may be defined as whatever tends to create belief. This proof may encompass anything from the speaker's appearance, apparent sincerity, and tone of voice to the speech itself. But since every speaker tries to appear sincere and interested in the subject, the debate situation focuses attention on the speech. Hence, for all practical purposes, the term *proof* means for the debater those items of evidence and reasoning that tend to make an audience agree with the assertions. *Evidence* can be defined as matters of fact or opinion that tend to support those assertions.

On the other hand, *reasoning* is the process of inferring relationships between the evidence and the assertions. The mere listing of facts or the reading of evidence cards or the piling up of opinions, therefore, is not enough to create belief—the audience must be shown an explicit logical relationship between these things and the assertion at hand.

The Toulmin Model

Stephen Toulmin, a philosopher, rhetorician, and logician, has described the process of proof in terms of three areas that lead an audience through the reasoning process. He calls these areas data, warrant, and claim.

Data are the items of information you gather, remember, and process. You can think of these items as evidence in a debate. They can be the examples, quotations, statistics, or other materials you use to build up your analysis. On the basis of these data, you ask the audience to accept your *claim.*

The claim is the end of the reasoning process, and it is your conclusion or, in debate, your argument. Several arguments become the data for an issue, and the issues become the reasons to support the proposition. Thus, the debate is structured so that there are interrelated series of claims, each backed up by data. The way we connect these materials, our linking of ideas, is called the *warrant.*

The warrant is the reasoning process by which we look at one bit of information (data) and decide what it means (claim). Sometimes logic provides the warrants for our conclusions; sometimes the warrants are elusive, illogical, or even missing altogether. In a debate, the reasoning process is often overlooked when you search for problems with your own case or that of your opponents. It is easier to see data, and thus many debaters simply try to rely on or indict the evidence. It is also easy to see the claims, since they are the major headings of the case outline. Warrants, or reasons to connect information, are much more difficult to locate, and we shall encourage you to keep looking for the underlying reasons or assumptions you and other debaters use.

An easy way to think of the reasoning process in the Toulmin model is in the following diagram.

In addition to this simple introduction, Toulmin also describes limitations to the data, which might call for supports. There are also limitations to the claim: qualifiers and reservations about the extent of the claim or the circumstances under which the claim might not be correct. The warrant also may need to be supported. A good follow-up to this brief introduction to the useful Toulmin system can be found in many contemporary argumentation and logic books.

Burdens

Three more terms should be understood by the debater at this point: *burden of proof, burden of rejoinder,* and *burden of communication.* Each of these will be explained below.

Burden of Proof

The burden of proof is a primary rule of any argument or debate. It first requires the affirmative to bear the burden of proving the proposition. Subsequently, it requires every speaker to support every assertion made by that speaker. Because any assertion must be supported by proofs, "Those who assert must prove" is a fundamental and long-standing rule of every debate.

Burden of Rebuttal

The burden of rebuttal is the second rule of debate shared by all speakers. It requires that a speaker reply to an assertion that is supported by sufficient proofs. If opposing speakers do not reply, the audience may legitimately agree with the original presenter of the assertion and therefore reject the second speaker's case. The failure to respond may be taken as granting the assertion (and thus the argument or issue) to the original presenter.

Burden of Communication

The burden of communication is the third key term to be understood by every debater. We have already mentioned this concept in the previous section, but it bears repeating. Each speaker is obligated to communicate issues, arguments, and evidence to the audience. If the debaters are talking only among themselves, little good is done. If they use shorthand abbreviations, jargon, and incomplete references and citations, they are failing to communicate clearly to the audience. As with the other two burdens, each speaker carries and must uphold the burden of communication by following the outline format suggested; identifying the issues and arguments along the way through the use of clear transitions, previews, and reviews; and speaking at a tone and rate that enables the audience to follow and to respond.

These three burdens are carried initially by the first affirmative and by *every* speaker who follows. They are part of every debate proposition of fact, of value, or of policy in traditional, cross-examination, Lincoln-Douglas, or parliamentary format. The speaker who fails to carry every one of these burdens also fails to carry the debate.

As noted earlier, when a speaker advances a proposition for acceptance (for instance, that we should increase our highway building), the audience can merely raise the question "Why should we?" The burden of proof for the affirmative at that point becomes the necessity of answering that question. But after the affirmative speaker has presented reasons for the audience to agree with the statement, the audience in a sense turns to the negative and says, "Well, why not?" The burden of rebuttal initially falls to the negative, requiring them to answer that second question in order to prevent the audience from accepting the affirmative's position. Both teams must carry the burden of communication from the first speech forward. This burden becomes more difficult as the debate progresses, for the number of issues and arguments increases and the time limits shrink. Nevertheless, the burden of communication must be met for either team to have impact on the decision.

A final note of caution is in order before we turn to the uses of proof in actual debate. We defined *proof* as "whatever tends to create belief." A speaker dealing with a proposition of value is dealing with areas of subjectivity and relative merits. The speaker in a policy-oriented debate is dealing with future action, with prediction and forecast. Therefore, neither speaker can offer absolute proofs. They are dealing in the realm of probability, of reasonableness, and of comparative worth, not in certainty. Some debaters are distressed to find that their opponents offer arguments that seem just as good as their own, but this result is perfectly natural in a discussion that is essentially seeking a choice or judgment between two or more possible alternatives or evaluations.

[handwritten margin note: Probable or reasonable]

Obviously, then, no single argument in a debate is likely to be conclusive by itself. No single proof is likely to settle the whole discussion. Therefore, the debater must be prepared to use a wide variety of arguments and evidence to make sure (or more probable) that the audience will accept the overall case.

Therefore, as the debate speakers prepare for the debate, they face an extremely complex series of problems: understanding the debate proposition, outlining their own and their colleague's approach to the case, collecting proofs, and even anticipating attacks by the opponents. The problems are complex, but each speaker's preparation can be simplified if this entire process of assertion and proof is understood in terms of four elements involved in the debate.

Structural Elements
Structural Elements as Basic Concepts

Four structural elements serve as the ingredients of a debate case. They are (1) the proposition, (2) the issues, (3) the arguments, and (4) the evidence. Analysis of a debate case is possible only through a complete understanding of the function of these parts. A fifth quality, and the most important one, is the reasoning process. It, however, is not a separate element so much as the means by which the other four are bound together. The following paragraphs will define each of these four formal elements, while the subsequent section will apply each element directly to the complex problem of building a debate case.

Proposition. A proposition (or resolution) is a judgment expressed in a declarative sentence. Each debate centers on a carefully worded proposition so that everyone may know precisely what is being talked about. As we noted earlier in chapter 2, there are propositions about fact, value, and policy. The value or policy propositions are usually used in school debate, and both are supported by three formal elements: issues, arguments, and evidence.

Issues. Issues are often called inherently vital points. They are the conclusions that must be proved to establish that the proposition ought to be adopted. They are the main contentions that function as the basic reasons for the adoption of the proposition. Finding the issues relevant to a proposition is the result of analysis. Ordinary intelligence will suggest that if one advocates a change from the present system (status quo), it becomes necessary to support the idea that there is something wrong with the status quo or that some major new benefit will result from the change. In a policy proposition, if these faults or benefits are extensive, they may provide a sufficient and compelling reason for concluding that change from the present system is necessary. In short, the fact that change is necessary becomes an issue.

If you are dealing with a value proposition, then common sense tells you to provide your listeners with enough reasons to conclude that your evaluation should be theirs as well. Issues do not stand by themselves; rather, they appear as assertions and need to be supported with arguments and evidence.

Arguments. An argument is an assertion that is the result of reasoning. The characteristic feature of argument, in comparison with other discourse, is that it states or implies a reasoning process. For example, "The papers are on the table" is not an argument; but the statement "If we do not close the window, the papers will be blown off the table" is an argument because it contains an inference, the result of a reasoning process. Arguments serve as reasons for the acceptance of an issue. Arguments may stand by themselves with appropriate reasoning (as is frequently seen in parliamentary debate) but usually need to be supported with evidence.

Evidence. Evidence is that statement of fact or opinion that makes an assertion acceptable to an audience. In debate, evidence serves as a means to an end. The end may be called belief, conviction, or proof. Evidence has often been called the raw material of proof. Indeed, all relevant matters of fact and opinion should serve as the basis of every debater's reasoning. These carefully selected and cited facts and opinions are the debater's evidence.

Example: Functions of the Four Elements

In the previous chapter, you saw an example of an outline of an affirmative case on highways along with a companion negative outline on the same topic. Here is another example of a hypothetical case outline that uses the four elements in a value-oriented topic.

PROPOSITION: Resolved: That the United States would be justified in significantly increasing trade restrictions.

ISSUE: I. National security considerations would justify increasing trade restrictions.

FIRST ARGUMENT: A. Highly technical products reach our adversaries.

EVIDENCE: 1. Secretary of State testimony regarding loss of important computer advances to terrorist states.

2. Defense Department report on military equipment sold through third parties.

SECOND ARGUMENT: B. Technical losses endanger our security.

EVIDENCE: 1. Congressional hearing quotation regarding uses made of our

ᵇy others that have
ᵢ. security.
. from Joint Chiefs of Staff
ᵢg danger to our military
ᵢel resulting from technical
ᵢrs.
ᵢndustries need protection, for
ᵢxtile industry has been hurt by
ᵢrts.
Statistics on lost jobs in textiles due
to imports.
2. Et cetera

Thus yᵤᵥ   ᵢe how the relationship of each of these elements is present in a value-oriented topic as well as in policy
questions. The rule is simple—all propositions are supported by
major issues, and these issues in turn are supported by arguments, which have specific evidence as their supports. All of these
elements are bound together by reasoning—a fifth and ever present factor.

When you move to chapter 5, do not forget this relationship,
because you will need to create both affirmative and negative
cases from outlines and the format above gives you the outline
system to follow. You might also remember figure 3.1, which represents a schematic relationship among the four structural elements of any debate.

As you can see, the debate case is built on evidence or reasons.
Good supporting materials, in the form of fact, opinion, and reasoning that the audience will find compelling, are the foundation
of every debate case.

Where do speakers find good evidence? Which material do they
select for use? How do they record information so they can use it
later? These questions will be answered in chapter 4, which provides an introduction to the process of research. Use the method
described there to seek and record information about your debate
topics and any other topic you need to research. Many students

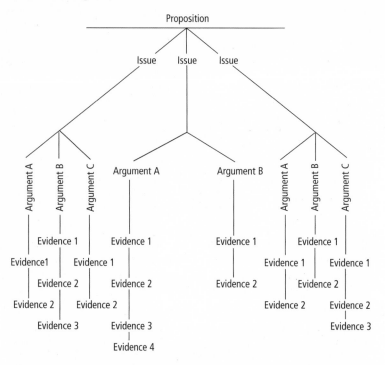

Fig. 3.1. Relationships among the four elements

find it beneficial to do essay examinations, term papers, reports in business and careers, and even master's theses and doctoral dissertations by using the research skills learned in debate.

The Relationships among the Four Elements

1. The proposition is supported by main issues, called contentions.

2. The issues, which appear as assertions, are supported by reasoned discourse, called arguments.

3. The arguments are supported with the best available evidence.

Research and Reasoning

4

Acquiring Knowledge
The Value of Research

Research is both a first step and a continuing process for the debate speaker. It is the first step in preparation because sound analysis of issues and arguments is possible only when the speaker has acquired a thorough background of knowledge relevant to the proposition. Initially, a debater needs to think about the topic: what areas are suggested, what terms need to be defined or analyzed? The implications of the topic area are important to think about and to discuss with others who are also concerned with the topic. Once this general grounding in the topic is developed, you can begin to focus your efforts. The following materials are offered as a guide to research.

Bibliographical Aids

The first step in research is to find the available references on the subject being investigated. The use of a bibliography is the most efficient method of discovering relevant materials. A bibliography is a systematic compilation of references on a given subject. There are at least three advantages to the use of a bibliography: (1) A bibliography tends to be a selected list of references that usually includes only the best material available. (2) A bibliography often provides an estimate of the value of a book or article by means of either an annotation or a reference to a critical review. (3) The compilation of an organized bibliography allows the debater to see the available references as a whole and gives direction to the subsequent research.

The debate speaker may ask how to go about finding bibliographies on a specific question. The answer is that the needs of the researcher have been anticipated and guides to bibliography have been compiled. These works are arranged according to subject headings and will indicate what bibliographies are available for the particular subject under investigation.

Reading

The debater should be guided by the principle that reading progresses from the general to the specific. This principle is based on the well-founded assumption that the investigator must have some grasp of the general problem before being able to intelligently evaluate its specific aspects. The method is consistent with other aspects of the debater's preparation: attention is focused first on issues, then on supporting arguments, and then on specific forms of evidence. Reading, therefore, begins with the best available general works (probably a standard book, together with an accepted research report), proceeds to references on specific aspects of the problem (probably articles in periodicals), and finally, surveys other books, articles, research reports, and newspaper accounts to accumulate specific evidence. If you are preparing to participate in parliamentary debate, you will need to continue this survey approach so you become an informed speaker on a wide variety of topics. A second guiding principle related to reading is that issues must first be discovered; next, arguments must be developed; and finally, attention must be centered on the gathering of evidence. An efficient practice is to survey each source briefly before beginning to read in depth and before taking any notes.

Note Taking

Because debaters cannot carry all their references with them (although some appear to be trying), they need to take notes on the material they read. Parliamentary debaters may be discouraged from bringing in specific items, so note taking will help them most in preparation sessions prior to tournaments. All debaters are thus immediately faced with the problem of knowing when to record data. In the process of research, the debaters will find that materials come in no logical order; an apparently valuable group of statistics may be encountered in the first general reference work that is read. At this point, the debaters may not know how the evidence will be used, nor will they be certain it is valuable. While discretion must be used, it is a good idea to record all materials that appear to be valuable. It is better to record too much than too little. The problem will diminish as the debater acquires a knowledge background in the subject.

Guiding Principles

1. Write your notes as though you were writing them for someone else.
2. Record enough information so that its meaning will be clear weeks and months later. Assume that your source will not be available to you again.
3. Record only *one* item on each card.
4. Use a consistent form that includes full bibliographical information. The format of the Modern Language Association is suggested as the standard academic system for footnotes, bibliographical citations, and paper formats.
5. Be consistent in the type of card you use for your notes. A four-by six-inch index card is probably the minimal size to be useful and is the one most debaters use in tournaments.
6. Reread your notes
   a. so that you will assimilate the results of your research. Such an assimilation of ideas will facilitate both the composition and delivery of your arguments during the debate process.
   b. so that items not useful can be discarded.

The importance of good note taking cannot be overemphasized. Your future success and progress as a debater depend absolutely on the quality of information you begin with. You base your analysis of issues, your development of arguments, and your assertions of support on the information you read and record. Accurate recording of notes will allow you to develop quality materials in subsequent work sessions. On the other hand, inaccurate or sloppy note taking can lead you to build erroneous assumptions later on, and if you present faulty information in a debate tournament and claim it is true and accurate, you may be forced to forfeit the round in which you used the erroneous evidence. You could even be removed completely from the competition or banned from participating in subsequent rounds or even future tournaments.

The penalty for using inaccurate evidence is so severe that you should be aware of it now and guard against any accidental misuse of evidence by ensuring that you take clear and accurate notes with complete citation. A note card might look something like this:

COMPUTER TRAINING HELPS WOMEN MORE THAN MEN
Joe Downing and Cecile Garmon, professors of communication at Western Kentucky University
"Teaching Students in the Basic Course How to Use Presentational Software"
Communication Education, v.50—July 2001, p. 228

"Undergraduate females tended to benefit most from each type of training. Across the entire sample, women gain more confidence using both PowerPoint and computers than men." (Study tested hands-on training versus reading the manual. Seventy-six students in sample, done in 1999.)

With such an index card, you can easily see what category of information you are dealing with and can instantly provide a complete citation for use in a discussion, in a tournament, or in response to a challenge, if need be. It is important to realize that *you* are responsible for all evidence *you* use, even if you did not personally locate or copy it from the original. If you have copied materials from another, then you become responsible for it later on, so make certain that you copy accurately and that you double-check the original as soon as you can. If, in a tournament, you happen to use a card that is inaccurate, it will do you no good to say, "Well, it's not my fault; I copied this from a teammate." *You,* not the teammate, will incur the penalty. Accuracy thus helps your friends when they review your materials, and if everyone on the team is following the same standards for accuracy and completeness, your entire team will benefit.

Interviews

After the debater has acquired a basic background of knowledge on the question, it is often helpful to discuss the problems under consideration with a person who has had special training and experience in the subject. Local colleges and universities may have such experts on their faculty, or there may be government offices, research institutions, or special interest groups who have personnel knowledgeable in the area. You may wish to make an appointment to interview the expert, and several members of your team might like to go. As in any good interview, a specific appointment, a series of well-thought-out questions, and plenty of notepaper and pencils or even a tape recorder will help you obtain a successful outcome.

Discussion

The value of discussion as preparation for debate can hardly be overestimated. In discussing ideas with others, the debater becomes aware of new facets of the problem and new ideas concerning the solution. And as a practical advantage, the debaters have an opportunity to exchange information among themselves. While a general discussion may be valuable in the preliminary stages of preparation, the most valuable discussions usually center on a particular aspect of the proposition for debate. A good "coaching session" may consist of a series of such discussions, each with a preplanned and announced topic area. That way, each debater can come to the session with relevant materials, ideas, questions, and contributions.

Organizing Materials for Reference

Debaters who have conducted careful investigation of the subject will want to organize and file the results of their research systematically. Careful organization at this point will facilitate the development of the case and will subsequently be of invaluable aid in the process of debate.

When to Organize. The organization of materials for reference should be delayed until the debater has a thorough enough background in the subject to see it as a whole. Until this point in preparation is reached, the debater is unable to apply useful sub-ject headings to the note cards. Preliminary headings should, therefore, be penciled on the cards and revised as the research develops.

How to Organize. There are two common methods of organiz-ing materials for reference. One method involves use of a loose-leaf notebook and arrangement of all the materials the debater will use—outlines of constructive speeches, an indexed section of evidence and rebuttal cards, and rebuttal note sheets—in one place. The notebook method requires careful organization but has the obvious advantage of keeping all the debater's materials in one place. An obvious disadvantage is that reading notes are most conveniently taken on index cards, which are difficult to incorpo-rate into the notebook system. Even the best of the currently available plastic sheets are often cumbersome, inadequate, or ex-pensive. The most common method is the use of a file box con-taining index cards and subject heading dividers. Some debaters use a combination of these methods, keeping their case outlines, rebuttal sheets, and most often used evidence cards in a notebook and the larger amount of remaining information in an accompa-nying file box. The more you advance in debating, the more you will develop a system that works for you.

What to Organize. Most debaters will wish to have two kinds of notes for reference. The first kind is the evidence note, an ob-jective statement of fact or opinion that may be used as the re-quirements of the occasion demand. Most reference cards will be of this type. A second kind of note is the rebuttal card. These cards are prepared in anticipation of arguments that will need to be refuted. By using rebuttal cards, the debater can prepare in advance what appears to be the best supporting evidence for an answer. In the process of the debate, the speaker who has pre-pared in this manner need not hurriedly think up an answer to an objection. Instead, the speaker merely reviews the thoughtful an-swer that has been prepared in advance.

A Comment on Debate Handbooks

As an alternative to research, some newer debaters may depend on the use of cheap photocopied handbooks that include affirmative and negative briefs as well as a grab bag of evidence. While many teams purchase these items, few use them to replace research. Debaters who confine their research to these predigested materials will lose much of the value of the debate experience and training. To be able to perform competent research on your own is a valuable skill that can be obtained only through experience. In addition, handbook users lose the creative pleasure of discovering for themselves, and the dull debating presented by these people reflects their lack of initiative. Glance through a team copy for ideas and formats and even to build a bibliography for your own further investigation. Handbooks can give you a start. But debate offers students an opportunity to master techniques of research that will be invaluable whenever they are called on to investigate, to analyze, to select, and to report. These calls are common throughout all academic undertakings and most careers that require intellectual activity. Handbook users lose this value. If handbooks are used wisely, they are probably hardly used at all.

You have seen some of the techniques for acquiring supporting materials, but how do you decide what to select and what to skip? One of the best ways to know what to do is to understand the nature of proof as it builds support for issues and arguments. The next section discusses proof and how you can build it out of your research and reasoning.

Developing Proof
Supporting Issues

In a debate case, each of the issues appears as an assertion. Together the assertions form a group of contentions that, if proved, ought to lead to the adoption of the affirmative proposal. Two formal elements provide the basis of support for the issues: reasoned arguments are the elements that directly support the issues; evidence is the raw material on which the reasoning is based. If you have followed the suggestions in the section above, you have begun to gather information, knowledge, and evidence about the topic. That information provides you with ideas, and in some cases, you have drawn or are beginning to draw some inferences or conclusions from this evidence. The following material considers the use of arguments and evidence as you get ready to construct your affirmative and negative cases. Whether you are debating a proposition of fact, value, or policy, the fundamental processes for reasoning from evidence are the same.

Arguments

Arguments appear in the debate case as reasons for the support of an issue. In the example outlined below, three arguments are used in support of an issue of need.

Example: Use of Arguments to Support Need Issues

I. There is a need to change from the present policy of nuclear testing and development, for
   A. The present policy is, in effect, an arms race, and experience indicates that the buildup of arms leads to war, for
      1. 1910–1914 example
      2. 1933–1939 example
   B. If the present policy continues, then the world population will be subjected to the dangers of radiation, for
      1. Statistical evidence
      2. Authoritative evidence
   C. Either testing and development are discontinued now or the dangers will increase and future control will be more difficult to achieve, for
      1. Many other nations will be in possession of nuclear weapons.
         a. Statistical evidence
         b. Authoritative evidence
      2. Inspection and control would therefore be more difficult and costly.
      3. The danger of the irrational use of nuclear weapons would increase.

The Fundamentals of Argumentation

The debate speaker may profitably spend a semester or more in the formal study of argumentation—the process of reasoning and analysis. The following principles are offered only as basic fundamentals and introduction to the terms that may serve as a useful guide in the analysis of argument.

Reasoned Discourse. The reasoning process puts previously unrelated facts and opinions (evidence) into a new relationship and from that relationship draws a conclusion. Each of the arguments cited is the result of such a process of reasoning. As the debate speaker presents assertions, together with supporting evidence, argumentative speaking or reasoned discourse results.

Generalizations. Although debaters will give a particular application to their arguments, nevertheless their reasoning will either assert a general principle or will be derived from a general principle. These principles are called generalizations. Such common assertions as "If Amy baked the bread, it will be good" implies the generalization that "All bread baked by Amy is good." The generalizations may or may not be sound. Perhaps the most useful guiding principle for debaters to remember as they analyze argument is that *every argument either makes a generalization or proceeds from one.* Inductive argument examines the real world of physical things or of human experience and makes a generalization about it. Scientific investigation, for example, proceeds from the observation of particular instances (examples) to the assertion of general principles. Deductive argument, on the other hand, proceeds from these generalizations and may or may not state the generalization on which the argument is based. The guiding principle for the testing of any argument is to find and evaluate the generalization on which the argument is based.

In policy debates, the descriptions of goals or the conclusions about how the current policy system works or should work are common generalizations around which the debate revolves. In value-oriented debate, statements of goals or value principles that people hold or ought to hold provide the generalizations for specific arguments.

Forms of Argument. The inductive or deductive argument may appear in a variety of forms. Nevertheless, because of the requirements for clarity in the organization of a debate case, the debate speaker usually states the assertions first and then proves them. In short, debaters usually use a deductive model for the exposition of their arguments. The previous example concerning nuclear testing used three forms of deductive arguments in supporting the need issue in a policy-oriented example.

1. "The present policy is, in effect, an arms race, and experience indicates that the buildup of arms leads to war." This generalization is termed a categorical argument because it asserts that all of one thing (arms buildups) lead to another thing (war). A way to state this categorical argument would be through the generalization "All arms races lead to war." If this generalization is dependable, then the argument is sound.

2. "*If* the present policy continues, *then* the world population will be subjected to the dangers of radiation." This hypothetical or conditional argument is different from the one above because it asserts its conclusion in a more tentative way than did the categorical one. It uses "if . . . then," which marks the argument as conditional. *If* the first part happens, *then* the second part will follow. This conditional or hypothetical argument could be stated thus: "If the present policy continues, then there will be dangers of radiation."

3. "*Either* testing and development are discontinued now *or* the dangers will increase." This third argument is called disjunctive because it asserts one thing will happen *or* another thing will happen. Disjunctive arguments are marked by the use of "either . . . or" in their generalizations. The underlying generalization for this disjunctive argument would be phrased "Either testing is discontinued or greater dangers will follow."

The three types of argument—categorical, hypothetical, and disjunctive—comprise the basic units of our reasoning process. In each case, whether you are arguing about values or about policies, you must draw the impact of the argument for your listeners. To demonstrate how your argument has value in their decision, you need to indicate the generalization from which your argument was developed. The value of any argument, therefore, depends on the quality of its base generalization. To grasp the generalization is to see the essence of the argument, any argument. Debate speakers are often prone merely to quibble about some third-level evidence supporting an argument when they should instead deal with the second-level—the argument itself or the primary basis for the argument—the underlying generalization. If you deal with the connections, or lack of connections, between generalizations, arguments, and evidence, you are demonstrating that you can debate about the reasoning process and about the errors your opponents may have made in that process. Such arguments are always more impressive and have vastly greater impact on the judges' decisions than do minor attacks on the evidence date or qualifications of a source, or any countersources.

This discussion is not to say that evidence is unimportant to the quality of your debating but to emphasize the fundamental place that reasoning plays in your thinking and communication of ideas. Once you have the reasoning process under control and can identify the links, or lack thereof, in an argument, then you are ready to fill in the supporting evidence as the third part of this chain.

The Relationship of Evidence to Argument. Arguments are based on evidence, whether that is the general knowledge a parliamentary debater brings to the debate or the specialized knowledge other debaters bring in the form of note cards and sheets of documentation. To reason in debate is to consider the meaning of facts and opinions. Generalizations emerge from the consideration of evidence—how you connect scattered ideas, facts, and opinions into a coherent series of justifiable conclusions. Fallacies, or errors in reasoning, result from drawing unjustified implications from the evidence. Because argument concerns the meaning of evidence, the manner in which facts are related to produce conclusions suggests different kinds of arguments. The four kinds of arguments stated below illustrate four relationships of factual material.

1. The argument from *sign* asserts that if fact A exists, it is a reliable indication that fact B also exists. A sign is like an announcement. The fact that Jo's car is parked outside her house may be taken as a sign that Jo is home. The sign argument is based on the generalization that all cases of A are indications of B. Sign arguments affirm that an assertion is true. The debate speaker typically uses argument from sign to establish that a problem exists or that a value is held.

2. The *causal* argument asserts that if fact A exists, it will cause fact B to follow. The fact that Jo's car ran out of gas may be taken as a cause for her car to stop. The causal argument is based on the generalization that all cases of A will be followed by B. These arguments are very strong if you can establish the connective link between A and B. Asserting such a causal link is easy, but proving it is difficult because so many B's in the world do not simply have a single cause A to point to; instead they frequently have a variety of causes.

   Causal arguments declare why an assertion is true. The debate speaker uses causal arguments to establish why the problem exists and why the proposed solution will work, or why a certain value structure exists and what the impacts of having such a value would be.

3. The argument from *analogy* asserts that if the facts relating to A and the facts relating to B are alike in certain known respects, they will also be alike in another respect. From the fact that Jo's 1995 Toyota gets thirty-five miles per gallon, the conclusion may be drawn that my 1995 Toyota will get the same mileage.

   Arguments from analogy are based on the generalization that if specific instances are compared and found to be alike in a number of essential and relevant respects, they will also be alike in others, particularly the one under discussion. The problem is that all analogies are ultimately false, for no two things or circumstances are ever exactly alike. If they were exactly alike, they would *be* the same thing. The debater must establish that the similarities are close enough to be significant. For this reason, analogy is best used to clarify or add interest as an illustration but is weaker to establish proof.

4. The argument from *example* is the inductive reasoning process that provides generalizations. These generalizations then become the major premises on which deductive arguments are based. After observing Jo wash her car each Saturday morning for six weeks, you might generalize that Jo always washes her car on Saturday mornings.

   The argument from example asserts a generalization. The

debate speaker uses examples to support general assertions on which causal and sign arguments may be based.

As you can begin to appreciate, these different types often are used in conjunction with each other. The interplay of types is based on the type of argument being offered and the type of support necessary or available. Let us look to supporting materials briefly.

Evidence

One test of argument is the evaluation of the evidence on which the argument is based. Evidence, as we have seen, consists of facts and opinions, and is the raw material on which the debater's reasoning depends. The function of evidence is to make the debater's assertions evident. You should remember a few guiding principles.

1. Use the best evidence available. It should be accurate, recent, reliable, readily available and verifiable, generally acceptable to the audience, free from obvious bias, and directly germane to the argument under consideration.

2. Use enough evidence to support your assertions clearly and yet have more in reserve.

3. Make your evidence clear by relating it explicitly to the assertion it aims to support.

4. Do not allow your evidence to be questionable. Ideally, the evidence should not be debatable. The facts ought to be as you say they are; the opinions ought to be the assertions of relevant authorities. A debate in which the speakers contest evidence is likely to be a poor contest; conflict should center on the meaning of evidence, its relevance, its impact, or its implications, not its accuracy.

Follow these guidelines in collecting and using evidence, and you will have a firm foundation for debating. Make certain that you examine your opponents' use of evidence on the same basis, and if they have been deficient, then you can cast great doubt on the conclusions they draw. Challenges about the accuracy of evidence are a rare and serious event in school debate. Most tournaments and associations will remove debaters from competition who use falsified information. Remember, if you say it, you are responsible for it, so make certain that any evidence you did not obtain firsthand has been verified to your satisfaction—to the degree that you would be willing to stake your debate reputation or career on its authenticity.

Debating the meaning of evidence is another matter, for it attacks the analysis of the opposition, not their trustworthiness or honesty. Many attacks that challenge evidence are really attacks on the interpretation of evidence and not on the honesty of the team involved. Be careful not to confuse the two.

As you can see, evidence is the foundation of good debate, whether that evidence is in the form of general information you have read and remember or in the form of specific materials you have copied onto note cards and have available during the debate itself. Good evidence leads to sound arguments, development of issues and cases, and good refutation. Good research generates good evidence, so if you follow the guidelines, even if they seem time-consuming at first, they will pay off as you begin to debate.

This chapter was designed to introduce you to the basics of performing research for debate or any academic undertaking. Some important suggestions about how, where, and why to do research were made. In addition, you were shown some initial methods for evaluating evidence and some ways to put evidence and conclusions together in a form called reasoning. The next step in this process is to put your analysis and reasoning into a format that you can support with the research and evidence you have gathered. The format is called a case, and the next chapter will show you how to organize both affirmative, or government, and negative, or opposition, approaches to a debate topic.

Constructing Affirmative and Negative Cases

5

In the previous chapter, we talked about the importance of doing high-quality research in creating your affirmative and negative positions. It is now time to turn your attention to constructing your cases. In a sense, you are always building a new case. As information comes to you and as you consider, analyze, and rethink your ideas and positions, you will constantly modify your cases. We will begin with the affirmative, as that position is more focused and easily grasped.

Constructing the Affirmative Case
Determining the Issues

Debaters who have acquired a background of knowledge relevant to the proposition are ready to organize the results of their research into a debate case. They should always begin by organizing the affirmative case. Remembering that the issue is the basic element in the support of the proposition, speakers should make it their first task to discover what the issues are. To do this, they use the method known as questionnaire analysis. Since certain issues must be established for any proposition, the questions that suggest these issues are stock, or standard, questions of analysis. They are generally called the *stock issues* of a debate proposition and vary slightly between policy questions and value-oriented questions. Each type of proposition will be discussed separately. Common to the types of proposition is the requirement that all affirmative cases meet the terms of the topic.

The *topicality* issue is the first test of every case and thus is mentioned here rather than in the development of the two subsections below. The question "Is the affirmative debating the substance of the topic?" must be settled before you go any farther. This seemingly simple question can take up the bulk of some debates, however, for analysis can differ. Topicality, as we see it, is not just the clear and reasonable definition of terms but the application of those definitions in a manner consistent with human experience. While we do not necessarily advocate the "ask the average person on the street what the topic is about" approach to deciding topicality, we do believe that the "ask the well-informed, educated community of persons who deal in the subject matter" approach is a way to test the reasonableness of the topic interpretation chosen by the affirmative. There should always be a variety of approaches to any debate topic, but if you select an interpretation that pushes the parameters of reason, you may find yourself having to defend the topicality of your case rather than its substance. For this reason, debate propositions that deal with policy issues are usually issued from a national committee with a description of parameters to guide debaters, their instructors, and their judges in evaluating the topicality issue. Value-oriented propositions are usually deliberately phrased in a narrow sense to provide some clarity and guidance. Even topics generated for parliamentary debates for a single tournament or those used in classroom exercises usually have some care and thought given to their phrasing so that the intention of the question being debated is reasonably clear. The general rule here is that no matter what kind of topic you work with or debate format you choose, you must develop a case that is clearly and defensibly covered by the resolution.

Analyzing Policy Propositions Through Stock Issues

Two general questions are appropriate to the analysis of any proposition of policy. The first asks whether there is a problem; the second asks whether there is solution. While these questions, by themselves, are too broad for useful analysis, they form the background for a more precise questionnaire analysis. Typically, five stock issues are used in the analysis of the policy proposition. One of the issues aims to analyze the problem; the other four analyze the proposed solution. The five stock issues are

    I. Is there a *need* for a change from the status quo?

       A. Does there exist a problem sufficient to warrant a change?

B. Does the problem exist as an inherent part of the status quo?
II. Does the affirmative proposal offer a solution to the problem presented *(plan meet need)?*
III. Is the proposal *practical* and *workable?*
IV. Is the proposal the *best available solution* to the problem?
V. What are the implications of adopting the proposal?
   A. Does the proposal itself have inherent faults that would create greater problems *(disadvantages)* than the proposal seeks to alleviate?
   B. Does the proposal have any benefits *(advantages)?*

In short, the stock issues ask general questions of a proposition in an attempt to discover the material issues, the inherently vital points. When the stock issues are thoughtfully applied by a person who has acquired a background of knowledge (through the research process suggested in chapter 4) about the question under consideration, relevant arguments will be suggested.

The following explanatory material is offered to clarify the relationship of the stock issues to the substance of the proposition for debate.

Explaining the Need, or Problem, Issue

The first stock issue asks, "Is there a need for a change from the status quo?" Analysis proceeds by asking two subsidiary questions.

1. Do sufficient and compelling problems exist to warrant a change from the status quo? It is presumed that no change should be made in present policies unless it can be demonstrated that problems exist in the present situation. Thus, the status quo has presumption—and the need argument seeks to demonstrate that sufficient and compelling reasons (problems) exist to warrant a change. This part of the need contention often turns on whether there is enough of a problem to constitute a reason for a policy change.

2. Why does the problem exist? Does it come from inherent flaws in the status quo? In developing the need issue, many debaters make the error of not going beyond the description

of the problem. They reason that a problem exists; therefore, the proposed solution should be adopted. In stopping at this point, they not only treat the need issue superficially but also fail to discover their most compelling kind of proof—that of causation.

The asking of the simple question "Why does a problem exist?" often leads to the essence of the affirmative need. When the debaters consider the reasons for the problem, they view the problem as an effect and the inherent faults of the status quo as causal factors. At this state of analysis, debaters may develop a compelling need for a change that is based on the inherence of the causal factors of the problems they discuss.

Example: Development of the Need Issue

Applied to a specific proposition, which we used in earlier examples, the result of the suggested analysis may appear as follows.

Resolved: That the federal government should adopt a new program for the development of the nation's highways.

I. The present system of state and federal highway development is inadequate, for
   A. U.S. highways are substandard for present needs.
      1.
      2. (Relevant evidence here will include a
      3. description of the problems, expert opinion, and
      4. authoritative documentation.)
   B. Expansion under the present system is not adequate for future needs.
      1. Public needs
      2. Private needs
      3. Defense needs
   C. While the need for adequate highways is apparent, the need for the federal government to develop an adequate highway program is the essence of the question under consideration. A main contention of the affirmative is that the present problems can be traced to a lack of federal development or, in short, to problems inherent within the status quo. Those problems are

1. Interstate rivalry
2. Unequal distribution of wealth among the states
3. Planning of much state road building to satisfy short-range political objectives rather than to carry out long-range interstate needs

---

Parts A and B in the example above are essentially expository. They describe a problem in the status quo. Part C is analytical, for it attempts to establish the reason for the existence of the problem. When both aspects of the need issue are established, they lead to the consideration of a solution. Attention now turns to the issues relevant to the solution.

Explaining the Issues Relevant to the Solution

Does the Affirmative Proposal Offer a Solution to the Problem? In school debating, the proposition itself states, in a more or less general way, the solution that is being advocated. The debate speaker must determine to what extent the solution ought to be enlarged and developed to form a clear plan of action. The practical question asked by the debater is "How important is a well-defined plan?" The answer is that it depends. Essentially, the importance of the plan depends on the nature of the problem. The resolutions that capital punishment should be abolished and that the United States should resume diplomatic relations with Cuba are examples of debate propositions for which detailed exposition of a plan of action is unnecessary. In these propositions, the plan is a procedural matter that may be regarded as not vital to the adoption of the proposal; the vital points concern the need for a change and the implications of change.

Other propositions advocate procedures that need to be clearly delineated. For example, with the proposition "Resolved: That nuclear testing should be abolished," it is important to demonstrate that the procedure itself—a plan for the abolishment of nuclear testing—will work in a practical way to put the proposal into effect.

Many propositions call for the establishment of a new institution—a federal world government, permanent labor controls, or national health insurance. With each of these questions, the affirmative speakers will be required to demonstrate rather con-cretely that their proposal will work in a practical way. Concrete-ness in the workability issue cannot be achieved without a tangi-ble solution—a clear plan of action.

This is not to say, however, that every detail of a plan needs to be discussed. The time limitations imposed on the debate speaker ought to suggest that such detail is not required.

The guiding principle here is that issues must be established, and the ability of the affirmative to establish the remaining issues depends to a large extent on the clarity with which the plan was presented. Often overlooked is that the essential manner of prov-ing a proposal is to apply it to the problem. If the proper applica-tion of solution (plan) to problem (need) is made, the demonstra-tion itself is a persuasive argument for the adoption of the proposal. This type of application leads to a consideration of the other stock issues.

Is the Proposal Practical and Workable? This element in the af-firmative case, generally called the *workability issue,* often be-comes the key issue in the debate. Depending on the nature of the proposition, the clash in the debate will usually center on the issue of need, the issue of workability, or both these vital points. While many affirmatives would like to be excused from the task of prov-ing workability, the advocate of change has a responsibility to es-tablish the workability of the proposal.

The first responsibility of the advocate of change is to offer a practical solution. It must not only be idealistic but also appeal to normal human experience. Practicality is a vital point, for a pro-posal may satisfy all the other issues yet be justifiably rejected on the basis of impracticality. For example, a proposal can be made both workable and beneficial by spending an exorbitant amount of money to make it so, but the basis of its workability may un-dermine its practicality. The general principle involved is that practicality must be judged in terms of its consistency with the human experience.

Workability means that the affirmative speakers must prove that their solution really is a solution. A solution in debate is a proposal that will solve the problems on which the need issue is based. If this application of solution to problem is not made, the affirmative is open to the charge of simply begging the question or arguing in a circle. Because this error is committed by so many debate speakers, the principle is underlined here: A proposal cannot be justified on the basis of *a* need for *a* solution. A proposal can be justified only by demonstrating that it satisfies the need. The method used is to apply the solution to the problem.

Is the Proposal the Best Available Solution to the Problem? While this question usually does not emerge as a key issue in a debate, it is nevertheless vital in the process of analysis on which the construction of the case depends. It bears directly on two aspects of the debate: (1) the plan of the affirmative and (2) the possible use of a counterplan by the negative.

The relevance of the question to the affirmative plan may be summarized by saying that within the terms of the proposition, the affirmative faces the problem of tempering the desirability of its plan with practicality and workability. In short, the best plan may be not the one that seems to offer the most advantages but the one that best balances the advantages and disadvantages.

This question suggests a second matter of concern—that there may be an available solution to the affirmative need issue that is outside the terms of the proposition for debate. If this is so, the negative may offer that solution as a counterproposal. While the practice of offering counterproposals is somewhat unusual, it is nevertheless a part of debate and ought to be anticipated and prepared for by the affirmative speakers. A general principle that might apply here is this: Do not be caught by surprise.

What Are the Implications for Adopting the Proposal? This question also bears directly on two aspects of the affirmative proposal—the possible disadvantages and the alleged benefits. That both are important suggests that the affirmative speakers ought to consider all the possible implications of their proposal. To do so is, on the one hand, to prepare for negative objections that may arise and, on the other hand, to enhance the desirability of adopting the affirmative proposal.

The disadvantages aspect of the affirmative case is often called the issue of greater evils. It may emerge as a vital point in the debate because even if a solution is admitted to be workable, it may be justifiably rejected if it creates greater problems than it alleviates. The affirmative must anticipate negative arguments on disadvantages and be prepared either to demonstrate that the disadvantages will not occur or that they are more than balanced by the advantages.

It is, of course, a benefit to solve the problems enumerated in the need issue. If the affirmative successfully applies its solution to the problems, then the enumeration of benefits becomes more than an exhortation based on question-begging assumptions. Persuasive appeal is given to the enumeration of benefits that actually emerge as concrete results of solving the problems. Furthermore, a second kind of benefit may emerge that is not directly related to the need issue. These may be called *added benefits* and ought to be considered. Indeed, in the absence of great disadvantages, added benefits constitute a kind of need in and of themselves. Debaters often overlook the persuasive appeal inherent in the exposition of reasonable benefits. The debate speaker should be reminded, however, that reasonable benefits emerge from the strength of the preceding issues. While the enumeration of benefits cannot give strength to a weak case, it can add to the effectiveness of a strong case. Construction of a special case out of compelling benefits is called the *comparative advantage approach*. In this case, the affirmative focuses not on needs or problems but simply on a new plan and the compelling advantages that they allege will result. In the comparative advantage approach, the benefits must still be sufficient and compelling to warrant a change in the present system. Whether you decide to use this method or simply to develop added benefits to a standard need-plan case, the general principle is the same: all implications of adopting the proposal ought to be considered.

Summary of Stock Issue Analysis in Policy Debate

The functions of the stock issues in the structure of a policy-oriented affirmative are given in table 5.1. By keeping these stock issues in mind, you can question your case at each vital point in its development and can better question any opponents' cases once you understand how to do your own. Now let's turn to the analysis of an affirmative case and the stock issues in a value-oriented proposition.

Table 5.1 **Summary: Analysis of Affirmative Case Structure**

Stock Issues	Explanation	Questions to Be Asked in the Analysis and Refutation of Issues
I. Is there a need for a change from the present policy?	Since there are almost always some problems related to any policy or institution, this issue is generally the easiest to develop. The issue is hardly open to attack if the affirmative is allowed to base a need on the fact *that* problems exist. The *reason* for the problems is the essence of the affirmative case. The status of the issue is often one of quality or quantity. Is there enough of a need in either impact or amount?	Does the affirmative offer substantial evidence to indicate that problems exist? Does the affirmative make a fair analysis of the status quo with respect to all the available evidence? Does the affirmative relate the problems to inherent faults of the status quo? Do the problems enumerated constitute an adequate need for a change? Can the affirmative problems be solved within the status quo?
II. Does the affirmative proposal offer a solution?	The necessity of developing a concrete plan of action depends on the nature of the problem. The affirmative plan needs to be detailed enough so that its workability can be demonstrated.	Is the proposed plan consistent with the requirements of the proposition for debate, or does it limit the responsibility of the affirmative? Is the proposed plan consistent in itself? Does the solution suggest a clear plan of action, or is it vague?
III. Is the solution practical and workable?	A practical solution is one that is realistic in terms of human experience. The proof of workability is in the application of the affirmative proposal to the problems that constitute the need issue. The issue tends to become a question of quality: To what extent has the affirmative proved that its plan will work?	Has each point in the affirmative need issue been satisfied by the affirmative solution? Is the proof of workability assumed, or is it demonstrated by evidence and reasoning? Is the solution realistic?
IV. Is the affirmative proposal the best solution available?	The problem of the affirmative is to temper the desirability of its solution with practicality and workability. The negative is justified in advocating a solution that is outside the terms of the proposition. This is called a counterproposal.	Does the proposition allow for a better solution? Is there a better solution available but not under the terms of the proposition for debate?
V. What are the implications of adopting the affirmative proposal?	The affirmative must consider all the implications of adopting the proposal, making certain that in solving some problems it does not create new or greater ones. If the affirmative has proved its case, benefits naturally result. The affirmative should also consider related new benefits that go beyond solving the problems outlined.	What are all the implications of adopting the proposed plan? Would the plan cause other problems? Are the alleged benefits actually derived from adopting the proposal, or are they just solving the previously identified need areas? Must the affirmative proposal be adopted to gain the benefits?

Analyzing Value Propositions Through Stock Issues

Debating about values in a school setting over the past thirty-five years has brought about a variety of approaches. The following stock issues approach provides a foundation for you to begin the development of a value topic affirmative case. While others may phrase them in different ways, there seems to be relative agreement on several areas, which we shall call stock issues.

These issues can be analyzed through a question format much like that in the previous section. Remember that at the beginning, the affirmative must meet the issue of topicality before it can go on to any of the other stock issues.

Identifying the Value. Before beginning to write an affirmative case, you must decide what value or value system you will adopt and defend. Often, the phrasing of the resolution gives you the general perspective, such as "First Amendment rights are more important than any other constitutional right." Clearly, the affirmative must uphold the value of freedom of speech, religion, and the press, but they also need to explain why these are important. To do that, they will probably want to link those freedoms to other values, such as respect for human rights and even the value of life itself.

Setting the Definition. The affirmative would do well to define the terms of the resolution in accord with recognized value systems or statements or authorities that clearly link the affirmative's interpretation of the question to a value system. If this definition is consistent with a value system related to authoritative discussion of the subject matter of the topic, then they will establish the topicality of the case.

Setting the Criteria. The criteria are expressed early in the affirmative to establish a decision rule for the debate. The affirmative should suggest that the debate decision be awarded to the team that better upholds the dignity of the individual, for example, or better upholds national security or some other defined value. If the affirmative does not specify criteria for decision, the negative may offer their own.

Determining the Hierarchy. Values, like policies, do not exist in a vacuum so much as they exist in a relationship. We offer exceptions to our values or describe circumstances in which they would not apply. We often hold competing values and thus must assign them a priority relationship. This priority relationship is called a *hierarchy*. For example, we might think it a high value to help our friends when asked but would not assist a friend in copying answers on a test because we value honesty above helping a friend cheat on a test. Seemingly attractive values often conflict, and some value-oriented debates test that conflict through their subject matter such as "Protection of the environment is more important than energy independence." Clearly, both positions could be supported by nearly everyone, unless or until they are forced to choose between them. Then a debate develops about value hierarchy. The affirmative must place its case in a hierarchy and compare it to any competing values mentioned in the proposition or any reasonably brought up against it by the negative.

Applying the Value

Linking It to the Status Quo. The affirmative need to ask, "Is the value we are upholding a dominant value in current society, or ought it to be one?" The difference will help determine the presumption issue.

If the affirmative can demonstrate that their value and its placement on society's hierarchy is consistent with the present system, then they may claim presumption. On the other hand, if such a claim is not easily made or readily apparent, then they need to establish that it ought to be incorporated by society or moved to a higher rank on the social value hierarchy.

Linking It to the Affirmative Case. Once their approach to the issue of presumption is determined by the affirmative, they then need to link their value to an affirmative case. They develop contentions that show the specific applications of the value to circumstances as they are or as they ought to be.

The affirmative will probably spend the bulk of their time in the first affirmative constructive in this phase. They need to outline several areas of concern that demonstrate that the value they are defending is worth upholding and that support for the value meets the criteria for decision they put forth early in their presentation.

Developing Value Benefits. A third area the affirmative may develop is the projection of any positive outcomes associated with the adoption of their value. For example, if new ways of evaluating the present system or even new beneficial policies or programs could be shown to result from their value structure, then they could claim value benefits. These value benefits, in themselves, can become a reason for the adoption of the affirmative case and certainly can add an extra bonus to the affirmative position.

Impact of the Negative Case

This area of stock issue analysis asks the affirmative team to look at the potential areas of impact the opponents may develop against them and to construct a case so as to guard against these arguments. These areas will be further developed in the section below on developing the negative case, but the wise affirmative will keep the possible negative issues in mind while constructing the affirmative. There are two major areas to think about.

Burden of Rejoinder. Initially in a debate, the negative will carry the burden of rejoinder—the duty to respond to the opposition. The affirmative might wish to play the role of a potential negative team while they are outlining their case to discover the immediately apparent responses. The affirmative can then construct their case so as to limit these responses, or they can develop potential answers for use as rebuttal material. These answers can be formalized as rebuttal sheets as the team prepares for tournament competition. For the time being, the affirmative need to ask themselves, "Are there readily obvious attacks on these ideas?" If so, then they need to proceed to the next question, "Can these obvious attacks be prevented by rewriting the case?" If so, then they should rewrite as necessary. If not, then they need to develop responses for use in rebuttal, or if the attacks do not have a good defense, then the affirmative needs to consider reconstructing the entire case. Some affirmative teams have trouble admitting that their case has an easily attacked soft spot, or they may hope that their opposition will not discover their weak point. Championship affirmatives develop the ability to go beyond their ego involvement in a case and look at it objectively. They also realize that depending on the inability or ignorance of the opposition is a foolish and fatal wish. That attitude is like hoping no one else discovers a damaging piece of evidence that you have come across. Eventually, good research and good preparation will win out over wishes and hopes.

Significance of Value Objections. Value objections are similar in philosophy to the disadvantages offered against policy ideas. "What new problems or difficulties would be expected from the adoption of the affirmative position?" is the question the affirmative must ask themselves at this point. Are there identifiable consequences flowing from the advocated value that could be significant enough to outweigh its possible good? If so, then the affirmative again need to respond to these possibilities by rewriting their case, preparing for rebuttal, or selecting a new approach altogether. More will be said about value objections in the section on negative cases, but the vital questions about them must be considered by the affirmative during the construction of their case to save themselves significant problems later.

Burden of Communication

While certainly a concern for every speaker, whether in debate or in other situations, communication of ideas is a necessary burden for a debater dealing with value propositions. The debate ballot commonly used at value-oriented debate contests specifically lists the debaters' ability to communicate their ideas as an issue to vote on. The founding of the Cross Examination Debate Association (CEDA) in 1974 was partly based on a desire to make school debating available to general audiences. More recently, the growth of parliamentary debate stems largely from this same desire. While many policy-oriented debaters and CEDA debaters certainly emphasize the amount and depth of their research, they too must be able to communicate the results of that research during a contest. While some specialized audiences may tolerate rapid, shorthand presentations, when needed, all debaters are expected to communicate their ideas and arguments at a tone and rate that a general audience of educated listeners could follow and respond to. In specialized settings, some debaters would probably be more concerned with reaching a specific audience of persons trained in debate theory and fully conversant with the debate topic under consideration. Thus, at the beginning, debaters on the affirmative need to ask themselves, "Am I communicating my ideas and arguments at a tone and rate that a general audience can follow and respond to?" as they develop their case. If they try to pack in too many ideas, too many subpoints, or too many citations of evidence, they risk losing a general audience. The affirmative in this instance needs to edit material out of the case. They may do this editing by deleting multiple evidence for a single argument when one is sufficient to make the point; or they may wish to focus the case to fewer ideas and issues so that each may be developed as need be. Debaters are always expected to present full evidence citation of their sources, and time must be allowed for that purpose during the presentation of the case. Attention to other factors of delivery will be covered in the chapter on presenting the debate.

Thus you have seen how answering several standard questions, whether related to resolutions dealing with policy or to value, can help you in building your affirmative case. In both situations, a general outline may be followed when you actually start to write your case.

Arranging the Affirmative Case

The process of putting the affirmative issues, arguments, and evidence together to make a persuasive debate speech will be treated in detail in the chapter on presenting the case. At this point in their preparation, the speakers ought to outline their case into three broad divisions: the introduction, the body, and the conclusion.

The Introduction. The purpose of the introduction is to make the proposition clear and to prepare the way for the constructive arguments. An effective introduction may have three parts.

1. An appropriate greeting, statement of the proposition, and definition of terms.
2. The statement of an affirmative philosophy, or general view, on the question. If debating a value-oriented proposition, you should also present your criteria for a decision rule in the debate round. This statement aims to give perspective to the debate; it relates the proposition to the area of national

or international concerns or values of which it is a part. An effective statement of affirmative philosophy is based on an analysis that relates the affirmative proposition to the status quo and provides the affirmative speakers with the broadest possible basis of persuasive appeal.

3. The preliminary outline, or preview, which provides an initial summary of the main affirmative contentions and serves as an effective transition to the main development of the case.

Body. This part is the main development of the affirmative issues, together with the supporting material. It will take up the largest amount of your time and should follow the numbering, sequence, and wording mentioned in the preview.

Conclusion. The conclusion should summarize the main contentions of the affirmative case and relate them to the proposition and the affirmative philosophy. When the conclusion is a succinct recapitulation of well-developed contentions stated in effective language, it will have a persuasive appeal in itself.

Now that you have a start in constructing an affirmative case, it is time to briefly examine the negative.

Constructing the Negative Case

Since the methods for the analysis and support of the affirmative case apply also to the negative, the detailed exposition of stock issues, arguments, and evidence need not be repeated here. It should, however, be clear that those who speak against a proposed change of policy or against the adoption of a proposed value judgment have definite responsibilities in terms of the issues, the arguments, and the evidence.

In short, the purpose of the negative is to refute the case of the affirmative. The negative speakers may choose to do this by means of straight refutation of the affirmative case, construction of a case for the status quo, or proposition of an alternative superior to that of the affirmative.

Straight Refutation

Straight refutation simply means a direct attack on the points of the affirmative case as they were presented. Depending on the phrasing of the topic and the affirmative's treatment of the issues, the negative may or may not base its refutation on defense of the status quo. For example, if a value-oriented resolution calls for the support of a new or existing secondary value over those currently in prominence, then a defense of current values would be called for and such a defense could form the core of a negative direct refutation. In dealing with a policy question, the negative would look at the affirmative development of the need issue and decide whether a defense of status quo mechanisms pertaining to the need area would be their basis for refutation.

While it is technically correct that the negative is not obliged to develop a constructive defense of the status quo, the concept of straight refutation as a method distinct from the negative constructive case is somewhat misleading. The difference actually centers on the method of presentation for the negative arguments. The negative refutation may be presented either from the basis of the affirmative's case development (following the affirmative outline) or from the basis of a well-developed negative position on the proposition.

Since the affirmative cannot win its case without establishing *each* of its issues, the strategy of straight refutation is sometimes to devote the whole, or a great part, of the negative's time to the refutation of a single issue. The strategy may be effective, but it has the disadvantage of limiting the negative attack.

Most often, straight refutation is a point-by-point attack on the entire affirmative case. The advantage of this method is that it allows the negative speakers to present a great quantity of objections to the affirmative case and may give the negative an initial advantage that is difficult to overcome. There are at least three important disadvantages to the use of straight refutation as a method of procedure.

1. Straight refutation focuses attention on the affirmative case as it was presented. The method often fails to place the whole burden of proof on the affirmative because it takes advantage of only those negative arguments that apply directly to the particular affirmative case at hand. The negative may thus fail to consider the underlying generalizations so important to a full analysis of the affirmative. As we mentioned in the previous chapter, a debate team that overlooks

the opportunity to debate the underlying generalizations
behind every argument misses the essence of good, insight-
ful debating.

2. The straight refutation of a poorly organized affirmative
   case tends to create a poorly organized negative. By simply
   adopting such an organization, the negative presentation will
   suffer from the faults of the affirmative.

3. Straight refutation often places the negative at a psychologi-
   cal disadvantage because people generally want the speaker
   to stand for something. If you wish to use straight refutation,
   we suggest that you combine it with the ability to analyze
   the underlying generalizations, the strategy of spending
   greater or lesser time on affirmative arguments as they warrant, the willingness to modify organization to make it coherent, and the presentation of a clearly defined constructive
   argument favoring the negative position.

The Constructive Defense of the Status Quo

The constructive negative approach is based on the idea that general analysis of the resolution will yield certain fundamentally
strong negative positions on the issues and that these negative positions ought to be introduced into the debate as constructive arguments. The method helps to make the negative position clear,
and it may place an additional burden of refutation on the affirmative. The method is based on a complete analysis of the present system (its policies or values) and results in a negative approach to the proposition that is analytical in nature. It focuses
attention on the strongest aspects of the status quo and places the
full burden of proof on those who advocate change. The constructive defense of the status quo may admit some faults while
supporting the position that these faults can best be corrected by
modification of the status quo (policy), or that the faults are out-
weighed on balance by the strengths of the status quo (value),
rather than by adopting the affirmative proposal.

The affirmative case is not ignored by a constructive negative.
Rather, a constructive negative ought to facilitate refutation by
allowing the negative to refute affirmative arguments within the
context of a clearly developed negative position. The result

should be a direct clash of affirmative analysis of the issues versus negative analysis of the issues. This clash is the aim of the constructive negative position. If it is even partially accomplished, it is clearly preferable to a straight enumeration of unrelated objections. The negative constructive allows the negative to develop a consistent philosophy; a coherent structure of preplanned issues, arguments, and evidence; and its own ground to support throughout the debate.

The Counterproposal and Counterwarrant

The negative may refute the affirmative policy position by admitting the need issue and offering a solution that is not possible under the terms of the affirmative's proposition. This negative strategy is called a counterproposal and includes an attack on the affirmative plan. It requires the negative to accept an equal burden of proof to demonstrate that its plan is practical, workable, and *more* desirable than the affirmative proposal. In a value topic debate, the negative may develop a counterwarrant—competing values not called for in the resolution—and attempt to show that these new values should replace those advocated by the affirmative. In both situations, the obligations placed on the negative, as well as questions in the minds of some judges about the very legitimacy of the approach, make these options unusual and risky for any but the most experienced debater. Our advice is to combine a defense of the status quo with judicious refutation of key affirmative issues. You may do this through both negative speeches or by having one negative speaker concentrate on the negative constructive while the other works primarily on refutation of the affirmative.

Arranging the Negative Case

As in the affirmative, a three-part construction will help you remember what to do as you approach the negative case.

Introduction. The purpose of the introduction for the negative team is to make its initial position clear and set up the arguments the team will offer. It will probably have three main aspects.

1. An appropriate greeting, restatement of the proposition, and reaction to the definition of terms.

2. The statement of a negative philosophy, or general view, on the proposition. In a value-oriented debate, this section should also include a response to the criteria, if offered, and a negative perspective on the debate. As with the affirmative, this statement should relate the negative position to the values, attitudes, or policies of the status quo and provide them with the broadest possible basis of persuasive appeal.

3. The preliminary outline, or preview, of the division of labor that the negative will employ—which speaker will concentrate specifically on which issues—and an initial summary of the main negative contentions in brief form.

Body. This section provides the main development of the negative issues and may be divided into two subsections. The first subsection may consist of supporting the status quo through negative contentions, while the second subsection may deal with straight refutation of selected parts of the affirmative case.

Conclusion. The conclusion should summarize the negative position on the definitions (and criteria, if the debate is value-oriented), the negative philosophy, negative contentions (if used), and negative position on affirmative contentions or issues. If this material is communicated in a succinct, well-organized manner, it may create an impression of a large barrier for the affirmative to overcome and thus will be persuasive to the audience.

This chapter looked at ways to begin your construction of the affirmative and negative cases and introduced you to the concepts of planning for refutation, as well as for defense of your arguments. Once you have begun outlining your affirmative and negative positions, you should review each of the questions mentioned and test your case with them. Then you'll be ready to consider in depth how to refute another's case—which is the subject of the next chapter.

Refutation

6

Refutation is the key element in debate and makes the whole process exciting by relating ideas and arguments from one team to those of the other. It is challenging because it is more spontaneous than reading prepared speeches. Refutation is based on research, constructive development, and anticipation of potential attacks. It is the essence of debate and is difficult to master. A great deal of practice and attention to the basic principles outlined in this chapter will help guide you to becoming an effective debater through skilled refutation.

The Purpose of Refutation

In good debates, sound constructive arguments will be presented on both sides of the proposition. The debate is won by the speakers who most effectively refute the opposition and most ably defend their own case. Therefore, attention to the complex task of refutation and defense will add much to the debate speaker's effectiveness. This chapter is based on the idea that the best preparation for refutation and defense is complete thoroughness at each step in the development of the debate case. In short, the most effective refutation is derived from a strong constructive case.

Indirect and Direct Refutation

Considerable confusion has centered on the word *refutation* because it is a broad term that is usually given a narrow application. The end, or purpose, of refutation is implicit in its definition: refutation is the attempt to demonstrate the error or inadequacy of the opponents' case. It is clear that the end of refutation is to destroy; the means utilized may be indirect or direct. Because debate is a unified process of persuasion, you can see that refutation occurs indirectly in constructive arguments and directly as the responsibility of meeting particular shifts of argument from the negative back to the affirmative.

Indirect

Debaters refute through an indirect means when they use counter-argument to attack the case of the opponent. Counterargument is the demonstration of such a high degree of probability for your conclusions that the opposing view loses its probability and is rejected. For example, the affirmative need issue may be supported by arguments A, B, and C. Negative refutation of the need issue may be the development of arguments X, Y, and Z. Although the refutation for the argument is indirect, there is a direct clash on the need issue. The use of counterargument is the strategy of the constructive negative case.

Direct

Direct refutation attacks the arguments of the opponent with no reference to the constructive development of an opposing view. Direct refutation, for example, attacks the affirmative need issue by demonstrating the error or inadequacy of arguments A, B, and C. The most effective refutation, as you can probably guess, is a combination of the two methods so that the strengths of the attack comes from both the destruction of the opponents' views and the construction of an opposing view.

To conceive refutation broadly, think of the affirmative case as the refutation of the status quo and the constructive negative case as refutation of the affirmative. While you may think of a constructive case apart from the idea of refutation, remember that constructive argument develops largely from counterargument. There is, however, a difference between the presentation of constructive arguments and the presentation of arguments intended to apply directly to the particular arguments of the opponent. The former is part of that broad look at refutation and may be developed in advance of the debate through your analysis of potential opposing arguments. Because the latter task is done largely during the debate, it is one of the most complex the debate speaker encounters. It is the aspect of debating that is most often done poorly. In the process of debate, there is a confrontation between the affirmative view and the negative view. This confrontation may be easily viewed as that between opposing outlines. In this process, direct refutation is an important means of attack.

Using Refutation Effectively

We have just emphasized that refutation has both a constructive and a destructive means, and that while the purpose of refutation may be accomplished by either, it is most effectively accomplished by using both means. Refutation and rebuttal, attack and defense, are opposite sides of the same coin, and the methods used apply to both. Direct refutation demonstrates the error or inadequacy of the opponents' case, while defense demonstrates the error or inadequacy of the opponents' refutation. In both cases, the debate speaker's method is the same—building the refutation and rebuttal on the analysis of the reasoning process and evaluation of evidence. Let us now focus on direct refutation, the destructive means of defeating the opponents' case.

Methods of Direct Refutation

To refute the case of an opponent is to demonstrate the error or inadequacy of the arguments on which it is based. Because arguments are the result of reasoning about evidence, the two kinds of direct refutation are attacks on the evidence itself and attacks on reasoning (the meaning of evidence).

Attacks on Evidence

Since refutation aims to demonstrate error or inadequacy, the two broad tests of evidence are "Is the evidence correct?" and "Is the evidence adequate to prove the argument?" The following questions are offered as more particular criteria for testing evidence.

Testing the Facts

1. Are the presented facts consistent in themselves?
2. Are the facts consistent with other known facts, or do they appear to be unusual, "picked" evidence?
3. Are enough facts introduced to support the conclusions derived from them?
4. Are the facts accurate as they are presented?

5. Are the facts verified with good supporting documentation, and is the source qualified to know and report the facts?

Testing the Opinions

1. Is the opinion from a qualified source? Is the source an expert in the subject under consideration? Is the source prejudiced? Is this expert usually, consistently accurate?

2. Does the quotation cited give a fair indication of the person's real opinion, or was it "lifted from context" or otherwise distorted?

3. Is the opinion consistent with other assertions the authority has made?

4. What is the reason for the authority's opinion? Opinions are based on reasoning and are subject to the same tests of reasoning that apply elsewhere.

In summary, the refutation of evidence is limited to the questions of correctness and the adequacy of the evidence. Merely matching sets of evidence does not result in good debating. We believe the most common fault of debate speakers on all levels is that they are too often content to limit their refutation to a matching of evidence. For example, in a debate on the policy question of adopting a federal program of health insurance, the affirmative might argue that there is a need for compulsory health insurance and support this argument with evidence showing that in cities A and B, a significant percentage of the aged receive inadequate medical care. The negative might respond with evidence that indicates that in cities C and D, the aged are well cared for and thus no need exists. This futile matching of evidence results in an unfounded leap from the evidence to the issue. Argument, or reasoning about the meaning of evidence, is omitted. If reasoning is omitted from debate and if analysis is lost in simply comparing different piles of note cards, then school debate is guilty of poor education, as charged by its critics. The proper relationship of the evidence would suggest that some problems do exist, and subsequent reasoning ought to be along the lines of finding out whether enough problems exist to constitute a need, whether the problems are inherent within the status quo, and ultimately, whether the affirmative provides an adequate solution to the problems.

When a *New York Times* reporter assigned to the United States Supreme Court was asked to evaluate the debating done at a national debate tournament, his criticism was that the debaters tended merely to match evidence, not bothering to discuss the *implications* of the evidence. He suggested, not completely in jest, that the debaters simply match cards on each side of the resolution until one side ran out of evidence and thus "lost" the debate.

Evidence, of course, is absolutely vital to debate because it is the foundation on which logical argument is based. But on any debatable issue, there will be a wealth of evidence on each side. Matching evidence does not constitute good debating. Reasoning about the meaning of the evidence and the meaning of conflicting evidence, on the other hand, can result in debate speaking that has genuine analytical value. That is why it is still possible to debate an opponent's argument even when you may not have any specific evidence yourself. You can legitimately analyze and attack the faults and errors of the conclusions that the opponents have reasoned from their evidence. Often the strongest debating is not about the evidence but about the correlations among, connections between, and implications of the evidence.

Attacks on Reasoning

In good debate, the evidence is usually not questionable. The facts are as the speakers say they are, the opinions cited are those of recognized authorities, and each debater has a thorough knowledge of the evidence. Conflict, therefore, should center on the meaning of the evidence and on reasoning about the facts and opinions.

Since argument in debate is nothing more than the oral expression that follows from the process of reasoning, any debate speaker must develop skill in talking about the process by which conclusions are derived from evidence. In short, the question is "How does one talk about reasoning?" To answer this question, one must return to concepts introduced in the previous chapter. If reasoning can be described in terms of the relationship of the evidence to the conclusion, then the correctness of arguments ought to be measured with questions that test the correctness of that relationship. Table 6.1 is provided as a guide to the testing of arguments. In using the table, the reader should recall the guiding principle underlying all tests of argument—that every argument either is based on a generalization (deductive) or makes a generalization (inductive).

Applying the Tests of Argument

The foregoing materials demonstrate that the refutation of argument depends on analysis of the reasoning process. Debaters ought to apply the tests of argument to their own cases and make whatever further study they can of the process of argumentation. We strongly urge you to follow up with advanced readings in this area or even courses in argumentation, debate, critical thinking, or logic.

Common Errors in Reasoning

Before leaving the analysis of argument, the debater's attention should be directed to three fallacies, or errors in reasoning, that often occur in school debating. These are the fallacies of question begging, of extension, and of hasty generalization. While there are other fallacies, some of which are subunits of these three, we believe that understanding these major errors will help you right away in building good reasoning skills and, later, in understanding and avoiding the other errors.

Question Begging

The error of the question-begging argument is that it assumes the essential point that it ought to prove. For example, Jo argues that engineering students should not have to waste their time taking liberal arts courses. It may be agreed that engineering students (or any student) ought not waste their time, but the essential point to be established with reasoning and evidence is that liberal arts courses are a waste of time for engineering students. Beware of the unsupported assumption. Furthermore, the question-begging error may pertain to the whole case. Many debate teachers are alarmed by how frequently they encounter an affirmative case

Table 6.1 **Analysis of Argument**

Kind of Argument	Explanation	Example	Tests
Sign	The argument asserts that the presence of A indicates the presence of B.	A buildup of troops in North Korea indicates hostile intentions toward South Korea.	Is the sign adequate to prove the conclusion, or are other signs necessary for corroboration? (The probability of an argument from sign is strengthened as additional signs are introduced to support the conclusion.) Have unusual circumstances occurred that change the normal sign relationship? (The buildup of troops may be relevant to the internal affairs of N. Korea, or S. Korea may have staged a troop buildup first.)
Causal	The argument asserts that if fact A exists, it will cause fact B to follow. Or in past fact, A was followed by B; therefore, A was the cause of B.	Future fact: The invasion of South Korea would lead to a general war in Asia. Past fact: During the past three Republican administrations, there have been wars; therefore Republican administrations cause war.	Is the cause adequate to produce the alleged effect? Will other factors alter the alleged cause-effect relationship? In past fact, is the cause directly related to the alleged effect, or could there have been other causes for the same effect?
Analogous	The argument asserts that if facts relating to A and facts relating to B are alike in some essential respects, they will be alike in at least one other essential respect.	The war in South Korea was fought as a limited war, with characteristics A, B and C; so it follows that a war in Laos would also exhibit characteristics A, B, and C.	Are the cases really alike in essential respects? Are enough comparisons made to support the probability of the conclusion?
Example	This is the inductive form of reasoning that provides the generalizations on which deductive argument is based.	A buildup of troops in Vietnam, Burma, North Korea, and Laos each led to war; therefore, all such cases of troop buildup lead to war.	Are enough examples given to justify the generalization that is made? Are the examples clearly related to the generalization? (Are the examples really instances of the circumstances being generalized?)

that is based on question begging. In practice, the erroneous reasoning goes like this.

1. Problems exist that constitute a need for a change.
2. Therefore the affirmative proposal should be adopted.
   or
1. The values of the current system have faults.
2. Therefore the resolution ought to be upheld.

The unsupported assumption here is that the affirmative case will solve the problems or respond to the faults. The workability or desirability of the affirmative cannot simply be assumed without begging the question. A similar error is called the *post hoc fallacy,* which assumes that because one event follows another event, the first one caused the second. An example would be when a debater presents evidence showing a decline in unemployment after the institution of a federal program and then assuming that the program was therefore responsible for the decline. Unless some direct link is demonstrated, the mere sequence of events is not enough to support the conclusion. These two problems stem from faulty assumptions that imply or presume a relationship that may not exist.

Extension

This error occurs when the debater exaggerates either the meaning of evidence to make it prove more than it actually should or the opponents' position to make it easier to attack. The error is avoided by learning to use evidence judiciously and by developing a sense of fairness and objectivity in dealing with the argument of the opponent. Many debaters get used to thinking about ideas, issues, arguments, and even evidence in a standard way, and often miss the meaning when an opponent offers a seemingly standard idea but with a unique slant.

The debater who is not listening carefully then attacks the argument that was expected but not the one actually presented. If you hear a negative speaker claiming, "This affirmative team would support greater freedom of information, thus making birth control materials easily available to high school students and destroying the American family," you are witnessing an error in extension. Concentration, good note taking, and listening skills will help you avoid this embarrassing error and thus help you avoid the fallacy of extension.

Hasty Generalization

A hasty generalization is the drawing of a conclusion about a group of instances when not enough of the instances have been observed. For example, if a speaker were to read a quotation that indicates that the public schools in Detroit have a 45 percent dropout rate and then conclude that "education in the United States is failing," you could easily see that this limited, and probably special-case, example does not provide enough information to support the generalization. It would need to be combined with some sort of national statistic to avoid the fallacy. Debate speakers who seek the dramatic appeal of broad, sweeping assertions are most liable to stumble over their hasty generalizations. Debaters who realize that they are dealing with probabilities and approach their subject reasonably and judiciously will take the time to establish dependable generalizations.

Summary of Principles of Direct Refutation

Direct refutation attacks the opponent's arguments and evidence to demonstrate their error or inadequacy. This attack is done in three general ways:

1. Demonstrating error by showing that the alleged facts or opinions either are not true or, if true, are irrelevant.
2. Demonstrating error by showing that even if the evidence is accurate and relevant, the conclusions drawn are not correct.
3. Demonstrating inadequacy by showing that even if the evidence is acceptable, it is nevertheless insufficient to warrant the conclusions drawn; or that even if the arguments are justified, they are insufficient to establish the issues.

Organization
Overall

Where should refutation be placed so that it will most effectively attack the opponents' arguments and ensure a direct clash in the debate? In answer, it should be said that clash will occur naturally in those debates in which both sides have carefully analyzed the issues and developed arguments in support of their position.

This is not to say, however, that either the second affirmative speaker or the negative speakers can read or memorize a pat speech. In the first place, all these speakers need to be versatile enough to avoid spending time on arguments that may already have been conceded. But most important, as the constructive arguments of the negative are developed, their relationship to the affirmative case should be clarified. The method is to present the constructive argument and immediately show the effect of the argument on the affirmative constructive case. This is effective refutation within the context of negative constructive arguments. The second affirmative speaker has the same obligation—to complete the construction of the affirmative case and, at the same time, to relate that case to the attack of the opposition. The most effective method is to answer the negative attack within the context of the affirmative case structure. The debate speaker who develops skill in this method will find that refutation will spring from strength.

It is easier for a speaker to return to and defend an argument or the entire case if the debate has developed from two opposing outlines. Keep your own outline in mind as you compare and contrast it to the outline of your opponents.

In short, the effect of placing one constructive case outline against another avoids the pitfalls of matching evidence but may result in the matching of constructive arguments. It may be argued that even this result is far more desirable than evidence matching. It should still be emphasized that the superior debate will not only demonstrate the clash of a clearly defined affirmative position versus a clearly defined negative position but will provide an analysis of the relationship of these two positions. Arguments will be related to those of the opposition so that the effect of one argument on another will be clarified.

The result to be expected would be smaller differences between the two sides, greater clarification of the key arguments on which the issues turn, and the tendency of the debate as a whole to move toward a more rational approach to deciding questions than the "right versus wrong" often heard when an affirmative opposes a negative.

Organizing Particular Arguments

Whether in the constructive speeches or in the rebuttal period, the debate speaker ought to view the whole case of the opponents and evaluate the effect of the total attack. Nevertheless, as the speakers talk about the attack of the opposition, they must limit the refutation to one argument at a time. While preceding paragraphs have stressed the importance of relating the particular refutation to the whole case, the intention here is to offer a guide to the refutation of particular arguments. There are five steps in the process of refuting an argument effectively.

Five Steps

1. State with absolute clarity what it is you are going to refute.
2. Clarify the relationship of the argument to be refuted to the attack of the opponent.
3. State how you will refute the argument.
4. Present your argument in refutation.
5. Indicate the effect of your refutation on the issue in question and relate that to its impact on the opponents' case.

In print, these five steps may seem to be cumbersome, but in practice they are completed briefly with the use of effective language. For example, the following refutation may be completed in less than one minute.

Example: Refutation

Here is a sample of what a negative speaker might say in refutation to the need issue of an affirmative case calling for a policy of permanent price controls. The speaker incorporates many ideas, and their relationship and impact, with an economy of words.

So, in summary, the negative has admitted that some problems could exist because of fluctuations in prices, but we have developed the contention that these problems do not constitute a need for the federal government to adopt a plan of permanent legislation to control prices. The negative reasoning has been based on the fact that there are now twenty-one state laws to control prices, in addition to ten federal agencies with price-setting authority. With this permanent legislation already a part of the status quo, the affirmative is faced with two obligations: (1) to demonstrate what is inherently wrong with the thirty-one controls now in operation and (2), of greater significance, to trace the present problems to a lack of permanent controls, because it seems apparent that the problems enumerated by the affirmative are not due to a lack of legislation. In short, the affirmative offers simply one more law to add to the thirty-one now in operation. They must demonstrate why this one will work.

What should the affirmative response be at this point? Do they give up and admit defeat? We hope not! Instead, the affirmative should adapt to the negative attack. If the above negative refutation occurred in the first negative constructive, it should be answered when it becomes relevant to the second affirmative speech. In this case, it would be relevant to the affirmative plan and its workability. The affirmative might say something like the following.

Before we proceed to the defense of the affirmative plan and its workability, remember that the negative has admitted that problems exist in the present system that ought to be solved. Their position is that future legislation will not be effective and should not even be tried because past legislation, which they defend, has failed. The negative position is defeatism, and if we all adopted their philosophy, progress would halt. However, the important idea for you to remember about the affirmative is that our proposal is better than any previous legislation, and it will work to solve those problems both teams agree exist in the present system. Let me now turn to the plan and show you how it is superior and thus how it answers the negative attack.

As you can see, the affirmative speaker has accepted the challenge of the negative in a confident manner and has previewed how that challenge will be answered. Notice that the speaker answers from the perspective of the affirmative case and concludes on affirmative ground. The speaker will now proceed to show how the plan will work to solve the problems and why it will work where others have failed. Well-prepared speakers will meet the opponents' objections by returning to their own case, their own ground.

Language

Because refutation is always concerned with the communication of rather complex ideas, it is highly important that the debater make the means of communication—language—as clear as possible. Avoid vague terms. Use the vocabulary of debate by referring to issues, arguments, and evidence. If the opponents have labeled an argument a certain way, use the same label when referring to it. Likewise, in your own case, use consistent references to your ideas and your outline in all your speeches. This care is not always evident, as table 6.2 indicates. These examples were taken directly from college debate speakers in a tournament situation.

Seven Guiding Principles

1. The most effective refutation is from a strong constructive case.
2. Evidence is refuted by testing its correctness and its adequacy as used.
3. Arguments are refuted by attacking their basis of support—evidence—and by attacking the reasoning—the relationship of the evidence to the conclusion.
4. Debate speakers must relate their arguments to those of their opponents to demonstrate the effect of the refutation.
5. The effect of refutation must be related to its impact on the debate as a whole. This relationship has three implications: (1) The refutation of evidence is related to invalidating or weakening arguments which that evidence tries to support; (2) the refutation of arguments aims at resolving the issues

Table 6.2 **The Language of Refutation**

Avoid These Expressions	Because	Use Instead
"The point has been brought up"	Vague. Calling everything a point, whether it is an issue, an argument, or evidence, is probably the most common language error in debate. By itself it is vague; when it is overused it leads to total confusion.	"The contention of workability has been attacked with the argument that"
"As our quotes have proved"	Vague. Be concrete by using specific references. The word *quotation* is the preferred noun.	"Both the data from the 2002 Rand study and the 2003 study done by Prof. White of Prestige University showed that"
"They said" or "We said"	Vague and clumsy.	"The first affirmative speaker asserted" or "The member of government claimed" or "The contention has been"
"The negative hasn't had too much evidence to support"	Clumsy. The use of *too* is sometimes called the "too tautology." It not only begs the question of how much evidence is enough but negates a circumstance that probably could not exist. Could the negative have too much supporting evidence?	"The negative has offered insufficient evidence to support"
"The status quo is taking care of" or "Our plan takes care of"	Trite.	"The problems are being effectively solved within the status quo" or "Those problems would be solved if the affirmative were adopted, for"
"There is no need"	Trite. The more judicious approach is probably that the need is insufficient to warrant change, not that there is no need whatsoever.	"While the negative can admit to some problems in contemporary society, these problems are minor and can be solved within the framework of the status quo. Therefore they do not constitute a need for a major policy change."
"The opposition's contention does not stand up"	Trite.	"The contention of the government has not been adequately supported" or "The contention has, therefore, been defeated"
"During my partner's stand on the floor"	Trite and clumsy.	"During the first negative speech" or "The Prime Minister's constructive"
"They came back and said"	Clumsy.	"The negative's response was"

Table 6.2 **Continued**

Avoid These Expressions	Because	Use Instead
"How did they hit this?"	Clumsy, although the use of an occasional question to clarify and emphasize may be effective.	"What was the attack on this argument?" or "Let's look at their attempt to refute this argument"
"The members of the opposition brought forth the argument that"	Clumsy; at best archaic.	"The opposition introduced the argument that"
"We stand on"	Clumsy.	"Our support for this argument has been"
"We backed this up"	Clumsy.	"We supported"
"Where is their proof?" and "We have offered proof"	Clumsy and erroneous. Proof is often confused with evidence.	"Where is the supporting evidence to prove" or "We have offered evidence to support"

of the debate in your favor; and (3) the loss of a single issue results in the defeat of the affirmative case.

6. Refutation must be clearly organized to be effective. Follow the five-step process outlined above for each and every idea you refute.

7. The language of refutation must be clear, concise, and direct. Avoid the common errors outlined in table 6.2, even though you may hear them used by others.

This chapter was designed to show how to attack the opponents' case through refutation. One of the ways to discover potential areas for attack is by asking your opponent questions about their case. That process of asking questions is called cross-examination and is the subject of the next chapter.

Cross-Examination

7

Before presenting specific guidelines for cross-examination, we will define and describe cross-examination as it is used in the school debate setting.

Cross-examination may be defined as the purposeful asking and answering of questions about the issues in a debate within an established period. An effective cross-examination will consist of a series of carefully thought-out questions that establish an order or a sequence of idea development that helps to persuade the audience to believe in you and your ideas.

Cross-examination was used at many high school tournaments but was relatively rare in college debating until the mid-1970s, when the Cross Examination Debate Association was formed and began to sponsor a nationwide series of debate tournaments featuring a cross-examination format. The National Debate Tournament then adopted a cross-examination format for its tournament, and shortly thereafter, cross-examination became a standard feature at virtually every high school and college debate tournament. The popular parliamentary style frequently allows for cross-examination or questions while the opponents are speaking. The time used in asking and answering questions is usually included within the speaker's allotted time. The Lincoln-Douglas format (one person on a team) also has designated periods of cross-examination. So every format of debate you are likely to encounter will have question and answer time, either as a specific time during the debate or as an interruption in the flow of a speaker. While these question and answer times may have some resemblance to the cross-examination done in the courtroom, they have their own goals, rules, and regulations. Each of these areas will now be described.

Goals

The primary goal of cross-examination is to persuade the audience to accept your position and reject that of your opponents. You can reach this goal through the purposeful asking of a series of questions designed to lead the respondent into statements or admissions that will have a persuasive effect on the audience. There are four means to accomplish the goal of cross-examination, and they pertain to both the person asking the questions (examiner) and the person responding to the questions (respondent). These means are to build your own credibility, to clarify issues in your opponents' case, to expose possible weaknesses in the opponents' case, and to build your skills of focusing on issues and responding to questions. Let's go through these areas one at a time and see how you can meet them.

Building Credibility

Persuade

You must be believed by your audience if you are to be an effective debater. Aristotle identified this aspect of communication more than two thousand years ago and called it *ethos*. By this he meant the way an audience perceives the speaker's character. In modern times, research has consistently identified four factors that influence the audience's perception of a speaker's credibility. These factors are dynamism, expertise, trustworthiness, and goodwill.

Dynamism. An audience will find you dynamic if you ask and answer questions in a positive, assertive tone. You should maintain good eye contact with your opponent and your audience. You should stand near the center of the speaking area when you are asking and answering questions, and use good techniques of facial expression and gesture as you would in any speaking situation. When you are listening to questions or to answers to your questions, you should remain courteous and respectful.

Expertise. To create a favorable impression of expertise, you should ask questions that reveal a thorough knowledge of the topic and that are directly related to the opponents' case. Likewise, your answers should show that you grasp the topic and have specific supporting material for your responses.

Show knowledge.

Trustworthiness. Trustworthiness will be communicated by being consistent in your questions and answers. You cannot change your case or your issues to avoid answering a tough question. The material you present in cross-examination should be of the same high quality as the material you would present in your constructives. If you do not know the answer, it is better honestly to admit you do not than to try to bluff your way with a low-quality smoke screen answer. You can always offer to try to respond during your subsequent speech (but remember you then *must* fulfill your promise or you greatly diminish your trustworthiness).

Don't Bluff.

Goodwill. Finally, goodwill can be demonstrated by both examiner and respondent by keeping the exchange at a friendly, professional, and issue-oriented tone. Good humor is appropriate; sarcasm and personal attack are not. Many debaters lose considerable impact (and thus points and possibly even the debate) because they do not distinguish between what they consider humor and what the audience perceives as rudeness. Goodwill is especially important when two teams are clearly at different skill levels. The more advanced team must remain professional and not fall into a superior or condescending style. In parliamentary formats, the way you rise and interrupt a speaker should be done with tact and a professional manner. Abusing the opportunity to interrupt the flow of a speaker by doing so frequently, having only superficial questions, or deliberately engaging in long-winded questions so as to use up the speaker's time, will be viewed by the judge as a violation of ethical or goodwill dimensions of credibility.

Humor yes. Sarcasm no.

If you keep in mind the requirements for building good ethos or strong credibility, everything else you say in the debate will have greater impact. Likewise, poor performance during the cross-examination can damage your impact in the rest of the debate.

Clarifying Issues of the Opponents' Case

The time for cross-examination is meant for you, as examiner, to clear up any possible areas of misunderstanding. Suppose you did not get a source citation for a key piece of evidence the opposition has offered. Cross-examination is time to get that citation so that you may then evaluate it according to the tests of evidence.

Likewise, you may have careful notes, but they indicate no evidence supporting an argument of the opposition. In cross-examination, you can ask, "What was the supporting material for your argument concerning the growth of energy conservation—contention II, section C?" If they did have some and you missed it, then you can avoid the embarrassment of saying later, "They offered no support for this argument!" when the judge and audience all remember that they did. Be careful in cross-examination, however, that you do not simply ask the opponents to reread or reexplain major sections of their case that you should have gotten the first time. Asking for repetition of an idea or phrase should be done sparingly as a beginner and probably not at all when you become accomplished at listening and note taking during a debate.

The cross-examination period is for the examiner to focus on the case of the respondent. It is not a time for the examiner to offer extensions of arguments that were forgotten during the examiner's speech, to bring up evidence the opponents asked for previously, or to argue with opponents over issues. It is the time to clarify your opponents' case, if it needs to be made clearer for your analysis to proceed, or to probe their case for weaknesses.

Exposing Potential Weaknesses in the Opponents' Case

This aspect may be the most exciting part of the cross-examination period. You can ask opponents to defend or justify their philosophy, their definitions, their case area and focus, their limitation of issues, their selection of arguments, their reasoning in drawing conclusions and connections, and their use of evidence. Again, your purpose is to expose not your opponents' potential weaknesses but rather the weaknesses in their case. It takes some skill and tact to avoid crossing the line between attack of ideas and attack of persons. This skill may be hard for beginning debaters, but we have seen advanced speakers who cross over this line as well. An easy way to remind yourself of the proper focus is to begin each question with a reference to a specific item or place in the oppositions' case, something like "My next question is about the first contention, in which you cite a twenty-year-old study to support your argument about new developments in technology. Given the rapid advancement in the technical fields, how do you justify supporting your argument with this evidence?" Such a question focuses on the analytical aspect of the use of evidence and really places a burden on the respondent without resorting to sarcasm, such as "How can you be so foolish as to use such crummy evidence! That mistake gives us the round." Such statements are to be avoided because they are more a personal observation than a probe of the opponents' analysis.

Another kind of question to avoid is one that makes it sound like *you* are the confused person: for example, "I don't understand your use of evidence in contention II.B." This is a statement about your own inability rather than a challenge for them to defend their case. Such beginnings as "I don't see," "I don't understand," and "I'm confused about" damage your own ethos either by making you appear weak or by being interpreted as sarcasm. Ask straightforward questions linked to an aspect of the oppositions' case.

Developing the Abilities to Focus and to Respond

These two skills are important in both asking and answering questions. When you are the examiner, plan carefully, so you can ask precise questions. When you have only three minutes to accomplish your cross-examination or when you rise to interrupt the speaker, it becomes important to be concise about phrasing your ideas. You might remember the examples above that begin with a reference to a specific aspect of the opponents' case. Avoid extraneous verbiage such as "Umm, okay, lets see now, I had a question here about something you may have said about, um, let me just think a minute." Your cross-examination time is precious. Work for economy in language and instead try something like "We question your conclusion on contention II.A, where you attempt to justify a 1,000 percent increase in taxes. Please explain how you arrived at the figure and indicate what evidence or analysis supports such a figure." This phrasing is direct, concise, and specific in its requirements of the respondent.

Also stay away from negative or double-negative questions ("Don't you agree that there is not enough energy in the United States?" or "Aren't your studies not applicable?"). These questions are also rhetorical, meaning that the answer is implied in the sentence, and they are really more statements than questions. Negative and double-negative phrasing is also logically confusing. The faults of negative questions and rhetorical questions are to be avoided. Ask straightforward questions.

Answer shld be direct & factual   When you are the respondent, try to be concise and direct in your answers as well. Some examiners will badger an opponent by insisting they answer yes or no to a complex or overly simplified question. If you can honestly answer yes or no, do so. If you cannot, say so and tell why. The respondent will not help build ethos by being deliberately evasive, and the examiner will not build ethos by obviously skewing the question or demanding an inappropriate response.

If the question is obviously relevant and germane, answer it with the same skills you would use to question another. If the question is open-ended, such as "Please explain your case," then the fault is in the question, and you may feel free to summarize your entire case from introduction onward. However, do not try *answer simply & directly* to dodge a question in anticipation of how it will be used. Answer simply and directly and from your own ground. ("We defend our analysis of that evidence because the conditions examined in that study are the same now as they were fifteen years ago.") We will now take a look at the types of questions that are asked in cross-examination.

Types of Questions

The four primary types of questions you will want to use are direct, open, probe, and leading.

Direct

Direct questions refer to a specific piece of information and usually require a short answer. Such questions as "What was the source for your definition of energy?" and "Do you support mandatory penalties for violations of your plan?" are examples of direct questions.

Open

Open questions allow the respondent to amplify ideas and probably should be limited to explanations of implications of the case rather than repetitions of ideas already presented. Saying "Tell us why you favor mandatory execution of violators" is better than "Explain your plan's philosophy." The respondent can then amplify and perhaps even reveal information that will help you develop a response later.

Probe

Probe questions are similar to open ones in that they require a longer answer than direct questions but are more limited than open questions. They are often directed at a specific line of reasoning that the opponents have used. For example, you can ask an opponent, "Why does the affirmative depend exclusively on federal government sources to support the need for federal intervention?" Such a question might reveal weakness in the research base of the opposition or lead to the development of a negative counterattack on bias in evidence. Trying to delve beneath the surface of *what* was presented to *why* it is included in the case may reveal significant ideas for refutation during subsequent speeches.

What's behind it all?

Leading

Leading questions are the stereotype from courtroom drama, in which the attorney sets up a series of questions that eventually lead the witness to break down and admit guilt or do something equally dramatic. The debater can likewise set up a series of questions, especially if some sort of logical relationship is the ultimate goal of the series. For example, the examiner might try something along the lines of the following example:

Example: Leading Questions
> EXAMINER: On contention II.B, what was your supporting evidence?
> RESPONDENT: We cited a study calling for federal intervention.
> EXAMINER: Was the study done by the federal government?
> RESPONDENT: No, it was done by Zwigler Research.
> EXAMINER: Did the federal government commission and pay Zwigler to do the study?

RESPONDENT: Well, yes, they did have a federal contract.

EXAMINER: What was the date?

RESPONDENT: October 1992.

EXAMINER: Was there a presidential election that year?

RESPONDENT: Yes, I believe so.

EXAMINER: Could money influence the results of a study?

RESPONDENT: I'm not sure what you're getting at.

EXAMINER: Suppose you were hired to mow somebody's lawn. Would you do it the way they wanted?

RESPONDENT: I guess so.

EXAMINER: Is it possible such bias might creep into a study report as well?

RESPONDENT: I suppose it's possible.

EXAMINER: Was President Bush running for re-election that year?

RESPONDENT: I'm not sure.

EXAMINER: Well, he was, and if we later introduce evidence showing he strongly favored federal intervention in this area as a theme in his campaign, are you still willing to stand by an argument whose only support is a fifteen-year-old study, done at the request and support of the federal government, which concludes exactly what the incumbent wanted it to conclude and which was issued just in time for the November election?

RESPONDENT: Well (pause), you'd have to show me where there's a problem.

EXAMINER: Would a reasonable person at least have cause to wonder?

RESPONDENT: Well (pause), I'm not so sure. (pause) We thought it was pretty good.

EXAMINER: Thank you; let's now turn to contention III. Can you restate your title of this contention for me?

As you can see, the examiner set up a series of questions designed to reveal a weakness in the opposition's case. While the respondent never admitted this weakness, most people in the audience would be impressed by the damaged credibility of the evidence and of the team that used it. They would be ready for subsequent refutation (not during the cross-examination but in a following speech) that attempted to discredit the argument and the issue it supported on the basis of evidence that might be outdated and biased. If this issue were a major one for the opponents, then it would be worth the time spent to reveal this weakness and set up later refutation. The sequence above would have to be a major objective of the examiner, for it takes about one and one-half minutes to complete. The time would be worth it for a major idea but not for a minor evidence challenge. Notice how the examiner used a combination of direct, open, and probe questions to set up a series. Effective cross-examination will have more than a series of single questions but will also be able to build on the answers.

The examiner can prepare in advance a variety of strategies based on the alternative responses that might come. For example, a well-prepared examiner will think, "What will I do if the opponent answers this way? What if they say this? What follow-up questions can I predict no matter which way the response goes?" Such advance analysis will keep the examiner in charge of the focus and direction of the cross-examination time.

The respondent can also prepare, in advance, possible answers. The best way is to work with your team members, ask each other the toughest questions you can about your own case, and practice giving responses that leave you on your own territory. As in refutation, the best preparation is a solid case that you have developed carefully, supported well, and know fully. In practice sessions with other team members, you can develop potential questions and listen to those developed by others. The use of videotape can be of tremendous benefit, enabling you to see yourself in both positions of asking and answering questions.

Remember, both examiner and respondent want to build their credibility by paying attention to the four factors mentioned above. They both want to clarify issues and ideas so that the basis for the debate will be focused. In addition, the examiner wants to probe the opponent's case and reasoning for weaknesses, while the respondent desires to defend issues, arguments, evidence, and reasoning.

Applications

It is possible to apply skills learned in the cross-examination process to nondebate settings as well. You can transfer skills in answering questions to your classrooms, where teachers often ask direct, open-ended, or probing questions about class-related work. "Did you read last night's assignment? What did you think about it? Would you like to see this area as part of the final project?" are examples of three types of questions that might be used in the classroom. Likewise, if you are tactful about it, you can employ questioning strategies to gain information from your teachers. Such inquiries as "What are the page numbers for tonight's reading? How do you rate the importance of this novel? Is this the type of item likely to appear on the final exam?" are ways you can use (and perhaps already have used) question skills in the classroom. By being prepared with both questions and possible answers to potential questions, you can become a more effective student and leave a strong impression on your teachers.

In the public involvement area, you may find yourself participating in community activities. You could use skills in asking and answering questions in such settings as civic meetings; club activities; council, board, and commission hearings; or those involving volunteer organizations such as civic or service groups. The ability to ask cogent questions and to respond on your feet is a skill that marks a leader and someone who will have an impact on the outcome of the meeting.

Careers almost always begin with interviews, which are largely question-and-answer exchanges. Most interviews will employ a variety of direct, open, and probe questions, so your practice in responding to them in the debate setting can prepare you to complete a successful interview.

Finally, many students involved in debate consider a career in law. Certainly the ability to phrase precise questions is an asset to any attorney, whether in the courtroom, with clients, or in interviews. Even if one does not wind up with the dramatic courtroom confession of television fame, there are still multiple opportunities to talk to clients, negotiate contracts, and interview parties in disputes. An important moment in the courtroom is when attorneys examine prospective jurors. This process, called *voir dire,* provides an excellent opportunity for you to observe attorneys using cross-examination skills and techniques.

Cross-examination skills are valuable in the debate setting and have wide application to a variety of situations in school and in other areas. All of these situations will go better if you are skilled in question-and-answer techniques.

You can see from this introduction that cross-examination is a major item in debate, even though it has only a few minutes in the format. Remember that it is not a time to argue but a time to discover ideas that you can later use for argument. Most judges will not remember what you specifically said or did during cross-examination unless you bring it up later. In fact, judges usually do not take notes during the cross-examination periods, so if you want your cross-examination results to "count," then you must bring them up during subsequent refutation or defense. *[handwritten margin note: Don't argue. Discover ideas & facts,]*

One area that is noticed by and remains in the mind of the audience is the impression you create during your presentation, especially during cross-examination. How you handle yourself while asking and answering questions, especially if you are interrupting a speaker in a parliamentary debate, will leave a lasting impression about your credibility. Remember to indicate to your listeners that you are dynamic, expert, trustworthy, and pleasant. Any other message runs the risk of downgrading your presentation and, probably, your score and your chances of winning the decision.

[handwritten margin note: materials for later on.]

In summation, three principles are important to remember.

1. The cross-examination period, though relatively short, can be critically important for setting up arguments that you will use later in the debate.

2. Most judges will neither remember nor apply what you say in cross-examination unless you bring it up again in subsequent speeches.

3. The manner of questioning and answering affects your

ethos. Communicate through your manner that you are dynamic, expert, trustworthy, and pleasant.

Until now, the principles we have discussed apply to all the speakers in a debate. It is now time to focus on the specific goals and obligations of each speaker position. Those duties are the subject of chapter 8.

Speakers' Duties

8

We mentioned earlier that wise speakers budget their speaking time with great care. There is good reason to be careful, namely that there is much to be done in a short period. But when debaters actually come to the platform to address the audience, they must also realize that each of the speeches and possible questions or cross-examinations in a typical debate is delivered under somewhat different circumstances. Obviously, the first constructive speaker has the full attention of the audience, while the last rebuttal speaker faces an audience that is probably weary and may be somewhat confused by the claims and counterclaims of the previous speaking or questioning periods.

Each speaker, therefore, may have somewhat different duties to perform in convincing the audience. The debate situation keeps changing, and the debater must adapt to those changes.

With the changeability of the debate situation in mind, we will now consider some of the factors each speaker should understand. The debate should be viewed as a sequence of opposing ideas—what the first negative says, for example, may force the second affirmative to revise a previously planned speech in order to meet the attack on the affirmative case. Therefore, it is unwise for a team to insist on a rigid time budget for speeches after the first affirmative. It is even more injudicious, however, for one team to ignore what its opponents have said—forgetting that the audience has heard those other arguments as well as their own. A sure sign of a poor debate team is a second affirmative who acts as if the first negative had never spoken.

The following suggestions are therefore intended as a guide rather than absolute time limits. The duties are generally the same in most debates, although there may be some room for adaptation as well. For example, in parliamentary formats, the speeches are

labeled to reflect government (affirmative) and opposition (negative) assignments. Parliamentary debates will frequently have only
a single rebuttal for each side. But the jobs of the speakers remain
similar, so each label will be used in the following descriptions.

Constructive Speeches
First Affirmative, or Prime Minister Constructive

This speech states the proposition for debate, defines any terms
likely to prove troublesome, and launches the affirmative or government line of argument. It is advisable for the speaker to outline
the entire affirmative case with great clarity, indicating which issues and arguments will be developed during the second affirmative constructive speech.

The first constructive speech, in short, should get the debate
started with a clear outline of the affirmative's philosophy in relation to the proposition with any related interpretations, limitations, or restrictions. Not every word of the proposition needs to
be defined: only those that may be ambiguous or that the affirmative understands to have a technical or unusual meaning in the
debate. A debate in which both sides quibble extensively about a
definition is usually won by the negative, since such quibbling dis-
tracts the affirmative from its job of proving the proposition.

If you are debating a value-oriented proposition, then this
speech must outline a clear value system to be applied in the
analysis. A debater dealing with a policy question must present a
compelling need or problem area, and often will indicate the plan
to solve that need.

Absolute clarity is the aim of the first speaker. Ordinarily, the
audience can get a clear picture of the whole affirmative case if
the speaker outlines for them the issues and arguments to be discussed and identifies any reserved until the second affirmative. A
clear summary at the end of this speech that reviews the outline
of the affirmative case as a whole will add emphasis to the case
and probably prevent confusion later on.

In chapter 2 we mentioned a possible time budget for this
speech. The exact time apportionment may differ from speaker
to speaker, but the important factor is that you plan each minute
of the speech. Take some time now to review that time suggestion

as you begin to write your first affirmative constructive. Remember that you need an introduction and definition of key terms of the proposition; a statement of the affirmative philosophy, including a value criterion if you are debating a value-oriented topic; an outline preview of the entire affirmative case, indicating which topics will be covered by your partner; presentation of the affirmative case, including supporting arguments; and a final summary of the entire case. Ideally, even if you will not be the first affirmative speaker but will take on the duties of the second affirmative, or member of government, you should still be involved in the writing of the first speech. You will have to defend it in the second position, so you must be completely familiar with its development and contents. Two team members working together can produce a document that both can then support.

First Negative, or Leader of Opposition Constructive

The duties in this speech are two: first, to state the opposition or negative's philosophy toward the proposition; and, second, to indicate the manner in which the negative will attempt to refute the affirmative's case.

In some respects, the first negative constructive is the most important speech in the entire debate. We saw earlier that the negative team must decide on its method of attack before the debate. It can merely refute whatever the affirmative says. It can attack the value system or offer an alternative. It can attack the need argument or the plan; offer its own substitute value system or solution, admitting a problem with the one in the status quo; or both. But once the first negative indicates which direction the team will take, the negative must follow through. They cannot come back in a later speech with another approach without greatly weakening their position.

Thus, the first negative speaker indicates the areas of clash. The affirmative speakers, after all, must create a belief in the truth of a proposition, using a number of subpropositions or issues at each step. Each of these assertions is like a link in a chain; if any one of them is broken, the chain ceases to exist. The negative usually chooses, therefore, to attack the weakest links in the chain of argument—to clash with those issues it feels best able to refute. A thoughtful affirmative will listen carefully to the first negative speech to determine the course of the negative attack and thus prepare its defenses.

Some negative teams will try to devote this entire speech to pure refutation, hoping to reserve their constructive arguments for their second speech, and thus outwit the affirmative by introducing constructive arguments, countervalues, or even counterplans late in the debate. Such strategy is of doubtful value, since essentially it avoids the real issues of the debate. Moreover, a practical time disadvantage is that the second negative speaker then has to handle refutation and counterrefutation while trying to squeeze the entire constructive argument into half a speech.

The first negative speaker also has the last opportunity to accept or reject the definitions offered by the affirmative. Silence at this point is assent. Some speakers say explicitly that they accept the definitions, and we prefer this approach to minimize confusion, but it is assumed that they are accepted unless otherwise noted. The affirmative has a right, logically, to make sure that both its opponents and the audience understand clearly what the proposition means—hence the definition of troublesome terms. But the affirmative is obliged to support the entire proposition as its minimal duty, and the negative should object to definitions that substantially lessen or alter the meaning of the proposition for debate. The key question in respect to definition, then, becomes "Does the affirmative or government define the proposition in a reasonable manner, or does it attempt to change it in an unreasonable manner?" Unless a significant change is made in a definition, the negative opposition should not quibble over it.

The first negative speech—and all speeches that follow—should at least acknowledge at the outset what the preceding speaker has said. If the first negative has no intention of spending time immediately on direct refutation of the first affirmative, it would be wise to preview for the audience the areas to be covered in the speech. In fact, a good initial preview is helpful in each speech. Without such an introduction, the audience may reach one of two conclusions: the speaker has failed to understand the opponents' arguments; or worse, the speaker is unable to reply to them. In the same way, any important material discussed in cross-examination or introduced in a point of information should be included with a reference to the fact that it comes from those periods.

Both negative speakers should make clear to the audience that the burden of proof for the proposition lies with the affirmative. The negative ought to make an initial analysis of the proposition in order to do this. Without such explicit analysis, the affirmative may (and many affirmative speakers do) get by with supporting a much lighter burden of proof than is their responsibility.

As the debate increases in complexity, laying out precise time budgets for the speeches becomes increasingly difficult. Start with the suggestions presented earlier, and as you become proficient in talking about arguments and issues, you will begin to make adaptations that suit you and the particular debate. Almost always, you will need an introduction, discussion of definitions, acknowledgement of affirmative arguments (and refutation if desired), and analysis of the proposition from the negative view—the negative or opposition philosophy, presentation of a negative case with supporting arguments, and a summary of both cases to this point in the debate.

Second Affirmative, or Member of Government Constructive

The major issues of the debate have probably been stated by the time the second affirmative, or member, rises to speak. The primary duties therefore will include reaffirming the affirmative point of view and concluding the case for the team.

The negative speaker has no doubt raised some objections, which the affirmative speaker must at least acknowledge. If desired, these objections can be addressed directly (and briefly) at the start of the speech. An alternative that we prefer is to mention them briefly in a preview, indicating that these objections will be discussed at the appropriate point in the affirmative case outline. We like this format better because it keeps the debate on affirmative ground and reminds the audience of the affirmative outline. Since this speech is essentially a constructive, the second affirmative must overcome the temptation to spend too much time on refutation while ignoring the support for the case. Any items discussed in cross-examination or brought up during point of information interruptions should be included here as well, with mention that they were initiated during those periods. These items may be brought up by either team but require response at the appropriate place on the affirmative outline. It bears repeating here that a key to persuasion for the affirmative is to keep the affirmative constructive outline constantly in the mind of the listeners.

It had been common in policy topics for the second affirmative to offer the solution, or plan, while the first affirmative concentrated on attacking the status quo or creating the need issue. Currently, more teams present the entire case in the first affirmative so that the audience can get the whole picture. While this change has resulted in presenting more areas during the first speech, each area has been given less time. Then in the second affirmative, the team can expand those areas that need additional support, perhaps presenting advantages as new constructive material. If the first affirmative, however, failed to convince the audience that there is a real, significant problem, it is useless to present a plan to solve it. Therefore, the first step of any second affirmative is to make a brief restatement of the affirmative case as a whole, acknowledging the negative attacks, and in policy debates, resupporting the need issue if it seems necessary. The effective establishment of the need issue then leads naturally to the development of a solution, whether that solution is presented during the first affirmative or held until the second affirmative.

On the other hand, in a value-oriented topic, the second affirmative may deal with extension of the affirmative case and refutation of the negative attacks. Usually, the practice has been to present the entire case in the first affirmative and allow the second affirmative to defend the whole outline. An alternative that some teams use is for the second affirmative to present value benefits they predict will follow from the adoption of the value they defend.

The alternatives above are largely a matter of personal or team preference or strategy. Judges may get used to a certain common practice in their area, so if your strategy varies from this norm, be especially clear in your initial preview of the affirmative division of labor.

The speech should end with a double summary, with the speaker restating both cases as they have appeared up to that point. The second affirmative needs a longer summary than the first affirmative because of the negative attack that has intervened. A practical plan for this speech might be a restatement of the affirmative case so far; acknowledgment (with refutation) of the negative attack; application of solutions or benefits, either as outlined by your partner or as new material; double summary; and analysis of the debate to this point comparing the affirmative and negative cases.

Second Negative, or Member of Opposition Constructive

The primary job of this speaker is to contrast the entire negative-opposition case against the entire affirmative-government case. This contrast is accomplished by analyzing the whole debate, centering the attack on the entire affirmative case, and evaluating it in terms of the negative view.

In many respects, the second negative has the freest hand in the debate, having heard the entire affirmative case. This speech can then be adapted to the specific affirmative in order to counter it. Material from cross-examination periods or points of information is also available for inclusion in this speech. The second negative should outline the affirmative case, then the negative case, clarifying the clash of issues and directing attention to negative arguments that the affirmative has ignored or failed to answer adequately. Finally, after development of the negative case, this speaker should recapitulate the whole debate as clearly as possible in a double summary and comparison.

Many debates are won or lost by this speech. If the affirmative has presented a well-organized, clear set of arguments, this speech represents the last chance for the negative to advance constructive arguments against it. Remember that in the rebuttal period, the affirmative has two advantages it did not have in the constructive: (1) it no longer bears the great burden of introducing and establishing constructive arguments to support the burden of proof and can, for the first time, concentrate primarily on refutation; and (2) the affirmative has the final rebuttal. During the rebuttal, therefore, the affirmative is on more than even terms with the negative. Hence, it is imperative that the second negative establish a definite superiority for its side. Moreover, since the first rebuttal speaker is negative, some of the effect of that speech may be lost when an audience thinks of it as a mere extension of the second negative constructive.

A practical plan for the second negative constructive is one that allows efficient comparison of the two teams' cases. This speaker could begin with an outline of the affirmative case and refutation of main issues on the basis of the burden of proof and then provide a restatement of the negative case, showing conflict with the affirmative. Taken together, these first steps constitute an analysis of the whole debate. The second negative can then apply the negative view to the whole affirmative case and provide a summary of both affirmative and negative, indicating conflict and the impact of the negative attack. This speaker must be especially careful to cover any new lines of argument that result from hearing the second affirmative. The first negative rebuttal can always continue previously issued attacks, but the second negative constructive is the last time to offer any new arguments.

Rebuttal Speeches
The Need for Clarification

Each rebuttal speech follows the same organizational plan, whether affirmative or negative. The speakers must criticize the opposing case and defend their own.

The rebuttal period can confuse an audience and even a trained judge, as well as the debaters themselves. Often, the most successful rebuttalist is the speaker who is merely clear—the one who is able to clarify issues for the audience and who shows at each point precisely how the arguments compare with those of the opposition. In a rebuttal speech, an accurate summary is often a decisive factor. Successful rebuttal requires a calm, crystallized overview of the whole case.

Discarding Minor Points

The prime virtue of the rebuttal speaker is an ability to reject, to discard, and to ignore the nonessentials. If you understand the main issues—and this depends largely on your preparation for the whole debate—you will know what is worth the expenditure of your time during the brief final speeches. Nothing is more futile than two debate teams quarreling, after forty or fifty minutes of speeches, about a minor point, such as the date of a quotation or the exact numbers in a statistical statement, but failing to discuss the impact of such information on any significant argument.

Thinking and Speaking in Outline Terms

It is essential that the rebuttal speaker think and speak in outline terms, thus making every issue clear. You can attack (or defend) conclusions, arguments, evidence or supporting materials, and reasoning. Time does not permit you to discuss every statement made by your opponents, so you must make a series of rapid decisions. If you and your partner have been making double summaries throughout the debate, most of those decisions will already have been made. Preparation for the rebuttal speeches has to begin, in effect, with your first mental summary of the opposition. It is at this point of rebuttal that careful listening proves its worth. And the rebuttalist owes it to the audience to speak in outline terms, constantly contrasting and comparing the major points to show where the clash occurs. You can in this manner help the audience make up its mind to reject the nonessentials and concentrate on the major issues.

Confusion in the rebuttals hurts the affirmative, or government, more than it does the negative, or opposition, since it clouds the issues and hampers the affirmative's attempt to create a clear belief in their proposition. But confusion may hurt the negative as well if the audience is unable to make sense of what the negative is trying to do. A confused audience may then remember only a well-organized affirmative case.

Emphasizing the Clash Between Cases

Emphasis in rebuttals should be on the clearly defined clash between the two cases. The audience is entitled to an honest comparison of the opposing sides. Any method that provides this comparison is useful, and any process that prevents it should be avoided. Hence each rebuttal speaker has the same purpose.

Splitting the Rebuttal Duties

Since it is still a debate between teams of speakers, partners should cooperate in their rebuttal speeches. Usually it is not advisable for each speaker to try to handle the details of the entire opposing case alone; lack of time will lead to a superficial coverage. Instead, partners may split the rebuttal job between them, just as they split their constructive case between them.

Duties of the first and second rebuttal speakers for each side differ only in minor details.

First Rebuttal (either side)
    1. Outline of opponents' case contrasted to own case, with statement of points to be handled by partner
    2. Refutation of at least half of the outline
    3. Summary and outline of partner's duties

Second Rebuttal (either side)
    1. Summary of entire debate contrasting both cases
    2. Refutation of remainder of outline
    3. Final summary of entire debate, pointing out the clash between the two cases

In parliamentary or Lincoln-Douglas formats, where each side may have only one rebuttal, speakers will need to combine all the duties above.

Listening to Opposing Speakers

One of the debater's primary duties is to adapt the case to the changing situation as the clash continues. Unless you are able to make an accurate judgment about the opposing arguments, you will be unable to adapt, so it becomes necessary for you to devise a careful, systematic approach to the problem of listening. Such an approach will not be difficult if you keep in mind the basic principle—that a debate is essentially a clash of opposing outlines.

A person listening intently to an ordinary speaker could simply make a single running outline, but in the debate situation, much more is necessary—the listener needs to know what the assertions are, what their supports are, what their relationship is to

Opposing Arguments		Reply	
First Affirmative/ Prime Minister	First Negative/ Leader of Opposition	Second Affirmative/ Member of Government	Second Negative/ Member of Opposition

Fig. 8.1. Debate flow-chart examples

the opposing case, and what possible replies might be made to key arguments. In other words, a full case analysis must go on while the opposing speaker is actually delivering a speech. Time is limited, so the method used must be both simple and efficient. In addition, it must be a system that can be used, without the necessity for recopying, to provide notes for later speeches in the debate.

The answer is an outlining chart that will give a visual comparison between assertions and the methods of proof used by the speaker. Any method that provides space for a good outline of the opposing arguments will be useful, but it is best to include a statement of proofs as well, so that the entire opposing case can be seen at a glance. If this procedure is followed throughout the debate, rebuttal speeches can be prepared directly from the analysis chart without recopying any material.

To keep track of the flow of the debate, some debaters use a simple two-column sheet made by drawing a single line down the middle of a blank page. Others prefer a four-column chart that is based on the same principle but allows the listing of all four speakers horizontally (fig 8.1).

This four-column flow chart is fairly useful, but unless very large sheets of paper are used, there is little room for noting types of proofs. The disadvantages of the four-column system are that

Table 8.1 **Case Analysis**

	Assertions	Methods of Proof	Comments
First Speaker	*Constructive* List here, in outline form, the major assertions of the opposing speaker.	List here, opposite each item in the left column, the proof advanced to support each assertion. Make a note of its type—for example, quotation, statistics, reasoning alone, or no proof given.	List here either 1. general comments opposite any item *or* 2. arguments you plan to use in refutation of each item. *N. B.:* It is essential to fill out the first two columns as you listen to your opponents. This third column may be used during your partner's speech or may even be left blank, since you will have to extemporize your reply in any case. The important point to remember is to avoid wasting time thinking up replies at the cost of missing a part of the opposing speech.
	Rebuttal *Repeat the process for all opposing speeches.*		
Second Speaker	*Constructive*		
	Rebuttal		

you may need to write in such small handwriting that it is not useful for speaking notes in later speeches, and large sheets are cumbersome when used for such notes. The main advantage of this system is that it can show all four speech outlines at a glance, matched horizontally.

The case analysis table (table 8.1) is another means of solving the problem of intelligent case analysis of opposing speakers. It would be wise for a team to prepare such a chart of its own case in advance, to provide instant cross-reference during the debate. The advantages of this type of chart are several: it focuses attention on the basic elements of assertion and proof, it provides quick reference to logical connections between parts of the opposing case, and it can be carried to the platform as speaking notes without any further changes. If you have outlines of your own case and that of your opponents, you are prepared to deliver an accurate double summary of both cases during each speech in the debate. Try these methods and discover which one or which combination works best for you as you advance in your debating skills.

This chapter presents some guidelines about the duties each speaker will have in a debate. Although there is some variation between the specific duties of debating value questions and those of debating policy questions, the basics are pretty much the same. One of the challenges of becoming a good debater is to learn about the duties of each position. You will be a stronger debater, and a better partner, if you try debating in each position, and we urge you to do so often.

Five principles related to speakers' duties are worth remembering.

1. Each speech in a debate has a different objective.

2. Each part of each speech has a definite duty to fulfill.

3. Budgeting of time is absolutely necessary to make sure that these duties are fulfilled.

4. Adaptation to the changing circumstances during the debate requires careful listening to opposing speakers.

5. All speakers must be as clear as possible about their own argument, about their reactions to those of their opponents, and about the relation of both to the debate as a whole.

Next we will try to bring together the final skill area needed in good debating: your ability to use effective language and delivery so that your good ideas will have both clarity and impact.

Language and Delivery

9

The essential idea to remember about debate style and debate delivery is a simple one: Debate, as the art of formal oral controversy, is a type of public speaking. Although *The Debater's Guide* cannot pretend to replace a course in public speaking, it might be useful to call attention to some fundamental principles that are common to debate and to other types of public speaking.

Verbal and Nonverbal Factors

As a type of public speaking, debate is an oral means of presenting ideas to an audience in an organized manner. Two thousand years ago, the Roman orator Cicero laid down three duties for speakers that are just as true today for the debater: to be clear, so the audience can understand what is said; to be interesting, so the audience will want to listen; and to be persuasive or convincing, so the audience will agree.

To accomplish these goals, language and actual physical delivery—use of voice and body to communicate verbally and nonverbally—are the chief factors to consider after the speeches are organized. And both are the means by which the debate speech is actually brought to the audience.

The Audience

Effective style (language) and delivery are impossible without careful consideration of the audience. Who are the listeners and watchers? What are their ages, their professions, their backgrounds? What are their prejudices, their predispositions? A set of phrases useful for a student audience might not create a favorable impression among an audience of bank managers. And the loud, gesture-punctuated speech that serves for an audience of a thousand people might seem awkward when delivered in a small room to only a few people.

There are two main considerations related to the audience—its character and its size. In general, the character of the audience affects the language to be used for maximal effectiveness. That is, since any speaker must use language that is intelligible to the listeners, any adaptation necessary because of the age, education, or profession of the audience will be made in terms of the language employed. Delivery methods are less likely to be altered for such reasons. A high school audience, for example, might not understand the term *reciprocal trade agreement* without some explanation, while a group of adult merchants would probably need no explanation. When in doubt about a term, use both the technical term and a synonym or a brief explanation the first time it is used in the debate. After the term has been explained once or twice, it can probably be used safely without further concern.

The size of the audience makes some difference in the type of delivery the speaker should use. If there are a thousand people in an auditorium, gestures must be made larger, facial expression will have to be more pronounced, and words must be delivered more slowly. Otherwise, some of the far-flung audience will not be able to hear or see the speaker. Before a smaller group, especially in a small room, delivery should be more restrained, because the audience can hear and see each slight change in facial expression or tone of voice. Debaters should especially avoid overloudness in small rooms. This advice is difficult to remember as the issues become more intense and the debate more active. Nevertheless, remember it.

The Judge as Audience

Most school debates are delivered before one judge, often a teacher, although there may be as many as three or five judges if the debate is one of the finals in a tournament. Occasionally, a debate may be delivered to a fairly large group of people, one of whom is to decide the debate while the others are spectators. To plan their speeches effectively, debaters should understand the true function of the judge. It is safe to say that the judge appears in the debate situation as a critical observer of your attempt to persuade an audience to accept or reject the proposition. This principle is extremely important because it determines not only the judge's position but the speakers' duties as well. It means that every effective debater must also be an effective public speaker.

Some debaters have the mistaken idea that the judge in a debate is like the judge in a courtroom without a jury, where lawyers stand up to deliver oral briefs. Therefore, they think, the ideal debater is one who merely delivers as many facts as possible in as short a time as possible, leaving it up to the judge to sort out all the pieces. Or they feel free to use a highly specialized jargon, as if all parties knew exactly what the words meant. Finally, these debaters feel that delivery is unimportant, and they merely read off long quotations in a dull monotone, looking down at their cards or paper and ignoring the people in the room. Such speakers will profit little from their debate experience, for they will find no real audience in later life that fits this false concept of the debate speaking situation. Indeed, most audiences would not tolerate that style with as much patience as many debate judges try to muster.

It would be better to think of the debater as a person speaking to a jury, under the watchful eye of a judge. In this case, both judge and jury require consideration. For this reason, the debater will address the debate judge as part of a larger audience. It is the judge's task to evaluate the job you do in persuading that larger audience.

The Language of Debate

Although it is impossible to encompass the complex subject of language in a few pages, there are three major ideas that the debater should keep in mind.

1. The language of debate must be intelligible to the audience.
2. It should be free of jargon and clichés.
3. It should, through the skillful use of transitions, help the audience to understand the progress of the debate.

Making the Language Intelligible. Most debate topics deal with complex ideas such as economics, value systems, politics, international affairs, or combinations of these. Therefore, the debate speaker enters into highly specialized fields of knowledge that may be unfamiliar to the audience. The first responsibility is to define the unfamiliar words being used—for instance, many audiences would be unfamiliar with the distinction between *preventive war* and *preemptive war*. It is also the debaters' responsibility to clarify terms to which they want to attach special meanings for purposes of the debate. For example, many policy debates have plans that involve a *commission* or *board* to administer the policy proposed in the topic. In a value-oriented topic, the affirmative may need to define a hierarchy of *more important* values. In either case, the audience is entitled to know what such terms mean to the speaker who uses them. A useful method in this respect is to link the word with a synonym the first few times it is used. In defining terms in the proposition itself, many affirmative speakers also find it effective to repeat the whole proposition after the definition, substituting their definitions for the defined words: "Resolved, that the State Department of the United States should offer to exchange ambassadors and other diplomatic representatives with the government of Cuba" (in definition of "Resolved, that the United States should recognize Cuba").

Once a term is used with a special meaning, it must be used consistently in that meaning throughout the debate.

How many terms need definitions? The answer is always a matter of judgment based on the character of the audience and its probable familiarity with the subject. Two kinds of terms almost always need definition, at least by synonym: first, terms that may be ambiguous because there are two or more possible meanings available *(tariff policy* or *environmental protection);* and second, terms with an ordinary meaning that the speaker wishes to use in an unusual way *(recognize* when the speaker means the exchange of only one ambassador and the prohibition of other relations, or *constitutional rights* to mean all rights contained in or inferred from the Constitution).

As a practical matter, in debates addressed to judges within a larger audience, the debater can simply define key terms at their first use and refer to synonyms for one or two times after that. Regardless of the audience, the speaker can never assume that any single statement will be remembered during the entire debate. Audiences may be inattentive or forgetful or may not understand completely the first time. Hence, you can see the value of repetition of important words and important ideas.

Avoiding Jargon and Clichés. Debaters sometimes live in a semantic world of their own, using over and over again the same stereotyped expressions. There is nothing wrong with using a technical term like *burden of proof* or *fallacy* if the audience is told what it means, since such terms can serve a practical purpose in the course of the debate. On the other hand, your originality will suffer eventually if you rely on a series of hackneyed terms without trying to think your way through more pertinent language. If adaptability is a key to debate success, then anything that restricts the freedom of language is a handicap.

In chapter 6, we listed some common clichés in refutation that occur during debates. A little attention to the speaking habits of debaters will no doubt reveal many more such expressions. For instance, some of the following might be noted.

Avoid	Because	Use instead
"my worthy opponents" or "the opposition"	May sound sarcastic; archaic at best; encourages antagonism	"the affirmative speakers"
"honorable judges" (in introduction)	Archaic; may sound sarcastic	"Gentlemen" or "ladies and gentlemen"
"I would like to run down the arguments of the opposition."	Ambiguous	"I would like to review the arguments of the affirmative."
"My partner has proved conclusively that"	Argumentative without further proof	"My partner has outlined the reasons for"

Using Transitions. Any debate can confuse an audience. Conversely, any debater who can clarify matters for the audience will stand a better chance of getting ideas accepted.

One of the major faults in school debating is a failure to make clear to the hearers the exact nature of the outline on which the team's case is built. Two speakers will sometimes spend fifteen or twenty minutes reciting statistics, quotations, and facts but will fail completely to show how all these things fit together. It is possible for a team to think in outline terms throughout the debate, assuming that the audience will somehow follow their line of reasoning; yet this same team may neglect to help out the audience with the use of verbal signposts that can do so much for clarity.

Why are verbal signposts so necessary in oral discourse? Their value is readily understood if one can imagine looking at a page of written language that has no capital letters, no punctuation, no paragraph indentations, and no boldface headings to indicate its parts and sections. The nature of oral discourse is even less clear as it strikes the ears of the hearers, since they cannot stop, pause, and go back two or three lines to try to pick out the main ideas. The only "punctuation" in a speech comes from the speaker. Consequently, and we have said this before, it is imperative to think and to speak in outline terms.

This advice does not mean that it is always necessary to say "Now I will turn to part III.A of my case." It does mean, however, that the speaker must skillfully utilize the ordinary transitional devices that keep the audience informed of the outline or organization at every step. As a general rule, a debater should never end one part of the case outline without telling the audience explicitly that one part has ended and another part is about to begin.

Any standard textbook of grammar or public speaking can supply a large list of transitional devices, but the debater should pay particular attention to three basic types.

1. *Transitions of Introduction*
   next
   another
   a further
   a second
   a third
   now let us turn to
   What does this mean?
2. *Transitions of Summary*
   in conclusion
   in summary
   finally
   we have now seen that
   these three facts (repeat them briefly)
   before going to speak about (next item)
3. *Transitions of Logical Conclusion*
   therefore

consequently

hence

we can now conclude that

thus

these facts demonstrate that

Any reminder or cross-reference is helpful to an audience. It serves as useful repetition that may help to drive home the argument.

Characteristics of Good Delivery

Delivery is the term we use to describe the communication of your ideas to an audience with words, gestures, facial expressions, and any other external means at your disposal (including visual aids). Mere recitation of words does not constitute good delivery; therefore, you should examine carefully the following outline of the characteristics of good delivery.

Posture. Posture should be natural to you and yet remain dignified.

1. Do not lean on desks, chairs, or the lectern.
2. Do not sway from side to side.
3. Do not stand stiffly in one position.
4. Move occasionally to provide variety and to release some of your natural tensions and energy.
5. Avoid positions that make you feel strained or tensely unnatural or that will appear awkward.

Position of Hands and Arms. Arms and hands should be held naturally but should never be fixed in one position.

1. Vary the position of your arms and hands from time to time to provide variety for the audience and further release your natural tension.
2. Do not lock arms behind your back or in front of you.
3. Do not do the same thing all the time. Change positions often.
4. Never attempt a gesture unless it feels natural for you.
5. Avoid toying with objects, such as pens, pencils, or note cards, and clasping or wringing your hands, since these actions will distract your audience from what you have to say.

Eye Contact. You should establish eye contact with the people in your audience.

    1. Watch the facial expressions of the individuals in the audience to see how they are receiving what you say.

    2. Make sure that you include every person in your audience, while paying special attention to your judge.

    3. Try to speak to individual persons instead of to the audience as a mass.

    4. Avoid looking out windows, looking over heads, and looking down.

Attitude. Your attitude (as the audience sees it) should be one of confidence in the value and importance of what you are saying.

    1. Show enthusiasm about the subject so that it will carry over to the audience.

    2. Have confidence in what you are to say so that you will have confidence in your ability to deliver the material as well.

    3. Avoid an appearance of arrogance or apology.

Voice. Variety in the use of your voice is the key to being clear and interesting.

    1. Slow down and stress key words when you wish to emphasize an idea.

    2. Speed up slightly when telling a story or listing factual details that illustrate a main point.

    3. Pause slightly between major ideas for emphasis.

    4. Vary your volume and your pitch to suit the material and the size of the room.

    5. Avoid monotones.

Above all, strive for variety. If there is one principle to be applied for effective delivery of a speech, it is probably this: Be varied—never do the same thing all the time.

Special Problems in Delivery

Some problems occur in debating that are not faced by the ordinary public speaker; other problems, like the use of notes, occur in other types of speaking but not in the same way. Following are brief notes about areas that pose special problems for the debate speaker: attitude of speakers, extempore ideal, memory and use of notes, speed of delivery, reading aloud, and visual aids.

Attitude of Speakers

Debate is controversy, and controversy often becomes heated. But nothing is gained by attempting to discredit your opponents. The debate speaker should show respect for opponents and for the worth of ideas. Debaters should display courtesy and fair-mindedness at all times. Certainly, it is not realistic to take a right-or-wrong attitude toward the debate—to act as if you and your partner have all the correct answers while the opposing team has nothing but ignorance and stupidity on its side.

Many close debates may be won or lost by attitude. Arrogance is the loser. Speakers should never forget that a good debate is an honest attempt to provide for the audience two different answers to the question posed in the proposition. The audience in entitled to make up its mind on the basis of a rational discussion of the issues, not on the basis of emotionalism.

Extempore Ideal

Adaptation is the key to successful debating. Every speaker who comes after the first affirmative constructive has to make some adjustment, and it is only the good extemporaneous speaker who can do so intelligently. The ideal is to know your own case so well, in outline form, that you can easily recall it to mind as you speak and thus adapt the wording of it to the situation at hand.

Memory and the Use of Notes

Extempore speaking from notes requires clear understanding rather than a prodigious memory. That is, wise use of notes can leave the speaker free to use personal phrasing for ideas, free to maintain eye contact with the audience, and free to use vocal variety of pitch, volume, and rate as appropriate. The only basic requirement is that the speaker understand clearly the purpose of notes. Notes are not simply small manuscripts to be read aloud.

The speaker who wishes to extemporize a speech—that is, to deliver a speech in a somewhat spontaneous manner based on careful, previous preparation of a body of material—will carry to the speaking platform two kinds of written material: an outline of the speech and items to be read aloud or referred to during the speech. In a debate, you should have your own case outline so well memorized that you will probably need to think only about the other type of materials. You should first settle on a standard size and shape for your notes—usually a four-by-six-inch note card is preferred because cards are interchangeable and can be easily rearranged to fit opposing arguments. Avoid flimsy sheets that tear easily or rattle audibly when held. Write notes large enough to be seen easily while speaking; if notes are too small, the card will have to be held in front of the eyes, thus distracting the audience and hampering eye contact.

If a speaker remembers to strive constantly to speak in outline form, then note cards will fall readily into definite patterns. Some cards will contain assertions; some will contain supports for those assertions. Others will give details of support. If the case is well outlined, it should be possible to lay out every card in a note file in its exact position in the outline. A note card that is difficult to classify means that the note refers to two separate issues (in which case, an extra copy is useful), that the speaker does not yet fully understand the case, or that the note card belongs in another section of the file for use against possible opponents or in building another case.

Speed

Some debaters, especially those who are still somewhat inexperienced, seem to believe that the ideal speech is one delivered at a machine-gun rate. Most Americans speak at an average rate of 120 to 150 words per minute. Thus, the debater who races on for ten minutes at 250 words per minute is going to attract attention, most likely unfavorable. A good delivery maxim is that the speaker should avoid any mannerism that calls attention to itself and away from the ideas. Consequently, it is wise to avoid seeming hasty and frantic by trying to cram a twenty-minute speech into the allotted time. It is of great importance to remember this guideline during the rebuttal speeches, when confusion is already probable because of the complex debate clash. Machine-gun delivery is often a sign of poor case analysis, because the debater is uncertain and tries to throw in every conceivable idea and fact in hope that one of them will work. Obviously, this speaker is unable to rationally decide which ideas and arguments are valuable and which are not. The intelligent debater selects only the best ideas and arguments before rising to speak and does not try to deluge the audience with a flood of words.

Reading Aloud

Reading aloud well is more difficult than it seems, because of the dangers to effective communication with the audience. Three principles of good delivery must be emphasized in reading.

1. The principle of emphasis: making the meaning of the text clear by stressing key words, avoiding monotones.

2. The principle of audience contact: keeping eye contact with the audience by means of constant glances, avoiding fastening eyes only on the paper.

3. The principle of variety of speed: varying the rate and the length of pauses, avoiding the tendency to accelerate. Most speakers tend to speed up while reading.

Visual Aids

Some debaters like to use visual aids—charts, diagrams, or objects—to clarify complex ideas during a debate. While their use is infrequent, graphs and diagrams could be useful for outlining complicated financial relationships, such as budget allotments for various parts of a program, or changes over time. If visual aids are used, however, they must be made available to both sides in the debate. They should be removed from sight after use but must be kept available if the other side wishes to discuss them during cross-examination or later speeches.

Visual aids have several inherent drawbacks and therefore should be carefully executed and well used. The user should keep in mind that clarity is the chief goal. The following hints for the use of visual aids may be useful.

1. Make the aid large enough to be seen clearly throughout the room.

2. In drawing, take care to produce heavy, dense lines

that contrast strongly with the surface on which they are drawn.

3. Eliminate excess detail.

4. Label the important parts, using heavy letters.

5. Consider differentiating functions or structures with the use of contrasting colors.

6. Check your use of aids in practice before you attempt to use them in actual debates.

Above all, then, the debater must remember to be a public speaker striving to secure acceptance of ideas by an audience. That is how you meet your burden of communication. As such, you must analyze the audience, adapting your language and delivery to the circumstances of the situation. The debate situation, as you have seen, presents some special problems that every debater ought to keep in mind. For instance, there may be a judge in the audience. Furthermore, the great amount of data usually presented in a debate makes it even more necessary than usual that the debater be absolutely clear, keeping the audience informed at all times of exactly what is going on.

The Ideal Debate Speaker

The Necessary Talents

Good debaters are speakers who can secure public acceptance of the ideas they propose, even though they are confronted by the organized opposition of others. Success under these difficult circumstances calls for a high degree of debate efficiency. As a final reminder, then, of the skills needed by the ideal debater, we offer you these seven talents to cultivate.

1. Ability to collect and organize ideas
2. Ability to subordinate ideas
3. Ability to evaluate evidence
4. Ability to see logical connections
5. Ability to think and speak in outline terms
6. Ability to speak convincingly, with clarity and impact
7. Ability to adapt to new ideas

Develop these abilities, cultivate them, and use them. Your debating and your future activities will improve as a result.

Appendix
Glossary

Appendix: The Stock Cases

Certain types of policy debate cases in CEDA and NDT team debate are easy to prepare and defend, since they follow naturally from any logical analysis of a problem. Even parliamentary debaters should become familiar with these stock cases for two reasons: first, because they will probably be the backbone of your own arguments and, second, because you must be prepared to refute the arguments of your opponents when they are based on the same lines of reasoning.

The stock cases concerning propositions of policy are based on one or more of the following types of argument.

Policy Topic Affirmative

1. There is a need for a change from the status quo because certain evils exist that must be removed.
2. The affirmative proposal is the change needed because it will remove these evils.
3. The affirmative plan will also give certain benefits or advantages besides removing these evils.
4. The proposed plan has no real disadvantages.
5. The plan is practical.
6. Other proposed plans or repairs of the status quo either do not solve the problem or create new disadvantages. (Since this argument may involve a lengthy process, it is usually held in reserve for refutation in the event that the negative offers a counterplan or a series of minor repairs to the status quo.)

The standard affirmative case in policy topics often involves the first three items above—a need, a plan to solve that need, and some advantages—although it is enough to simply have a need-plan. Another option in debate tournaments is the comparative advantage approach discussed in chapter 5. That type of affirmative has steps 2 and 3 as its core and then may add on any of those coming after. Our advice is to build as strong a case as research, time, and your communication skills will allow. Certainly, a well-prepared affirmative team will have considered all six items in developing a case.

Policy Topic Negative

The negative has a problem to solve before any approach can be made to an attack on the affirmative. The negative must choose one of the following lines of attack when dealing with a policy proposition, and it must stay with that line of attack throughout the debate.

1. The status quo is satisfactory. This approach involves defending the present order or structure of things and, hence, forces the negative to show how good it is.
2. The present system can be improved in minor ways to eliminate the problems. This approach involves admitting that problems exist but that minor alterations, rather than major restructure, are sufficient to remedy the situation.
3. Another plan (other than the affirmative's proposal) will solve the problem and is superior to the one offered by the affirmative. This tactic is the counterplan and involves agreeing with the affirmative that there is a need for a change and that a major restructure is required to solve that need.
4. The affirmative proposal is inherently flawed. This option may be combined easily with any of the other three for it is pure refutation. It involves spending the entire negative time in sheer attack on the affirmative case. Hence, the burden of proof rests squarely on the affirmative throughout the entire debate. In the other options, some initial burden of proof begins to shift to the negative as well, especially in option 3.

Some negative teams attempt to argue on all four levels, adopting an "even if" approach as a transition between each type. For example, they may start by saying that the status quo is doing just fine, then say, "But even if you think there might be some problems, we could suggest some minor repairs to take care of them." After that, they then might try, "Even if you don't think these repairs will solve the alleged problems, there is a plan we could offer that is superior to the one presented by the affirmative." The offering of conditional counterplans is tried by some teams, but many judges frown on this combination approach because it is difficult to focus on a consistent negative position. A negative team that combines any of these approaches takes on a large burden that may be too complex to communicate clearly to an audience. Our advice to beginners is to keep option 4 as a primary approach and then combine it with option 1 or 2.

The stock issues dealing with a value-oriented proposition were outlined in chapter 5 and can form the basis for a case construction.

Value Topic Affirmative

1. Identification of the value. This step is accomplished by defining key terms, setting criteria by which the value and the debate may be evaluated, and determining any hierarchy that might be necessary.

2. Application of the value. The value should be related to the status quo to provide a context and perhaps determine presumption. The value should then be explicated to the affirmative case to indicate how it links to the decision about the proposition, and finally, any beneficial results that follow logically from adoption of the proposition may be outlined.

Most affirmative cases develop along the lines of this two-part division. Thus they have subcontentions under each part that develop the subissues listed.

Value Topic Negative

1. Alternative value. The negative may identify an alternative value that they contend to be competitive with and superior to the one offered by the affirmative. Sometimes the proposition will provide this option in its wording. For example, "Energy is more important than environment" clearly tells affirmative debaters to support the value of energy development, while the negative is directed to support the value of environmental protection.

2. Alternative criteria. The negative may wish to offer different

decision rules for evaluating the hierarchy of values or the debate (see chapter 5, under "Analyzing Value Propositions Through Stock Issues).

3. Value objections. The negative may analyze the logical impacts of adoption of the resolution and offer objections as independent reasons for rejecting the proposition and the value it supports. These objections are not the same as direct refutation to the specifics of the affirmative case but rather stem from the resolution itself. Many negative teams prepare their value objections in advance of the debate on the basis of their independent analysis of the problems inherent in the value expressed by the proposition.

4. Straight refutation. As in policy-oriented debate, the negative always has the option to attack the affirmative case point by point.

Each of these options may be used in combination with any other to some degree. Our advice here is similar to that we gave to negative teams working with policy propositions. Number 4 is always appropriate and can easily be combined with any others. As you advance in experience and confidence, you may attempt other combinations that are appropriate to your level of proficiency and the approach called for by the topic or the affirmative case.

The options presented above are intended to serve as an introduction to the debate cases that are standard, or stock, approaches. While they have developed because they are useful in a variety of situations, they are not the only case formats. We suggest that you learn these fundamental approaches thoroughly before you attempt more difficult types. Beginning debaters should remember that there are no strategic advantages to be gained from trying to run unusual cases against other beginners. It takes great skill to present an unusual format, and if the affirmative case is not presented with clarity and precision, the affirmative will lose, not the surprised negative. Consult your instructors for suggested readings on advanced debate.

Glossary

AFFIRMATIVE SIDE. The speaker or team that undertakes to secure audience acceptance of the truth of the debate proposition.

ANALOGY. A type of argument that asserts that if the facts relating to A and the facts relating to B are alike in certain known respects, they will be alike in another respect.

ANALYSIS. The process of thinking through a subject and discovering the issues; systematic inquiry.

ARGUMENT. An assertion that implies the result of reasoning or proof.

ASSERTION. An unsupported statement.

BIBLIOGRAPHY. A systematic compilation of references on a given subject.

BLOCK. A brief of arguments, including reasoning and evidence, prepared in advance of a debate to apply against expected lines of opponents' argument.

BRIEF. A carefully prepared, complete outline of one side in a debate, including the evidence to support each point.

CASE. All the assembled proof available for determining the truth of the proposition (for the affirmative) or the untruth of the proposition (for the negative); the brief developed in full with analysis, reasoning, and evidence.

CAUSE. A type of argument that asserts that if fact A occurs, fact B will necessarily follow from it.

CEDA. The Cross Examination Debate Association, a national organization with the purpose of promoting educational debate and dedicated to teaching the principles of persuasive and communicative argumentation. CEDA selects debate propositions, frequently concerning values, for debate at approved tournaments and compiles rankings of schools on the basis of performance at those tournaments.

CLASH. The direct opposition between the affirmative and the negative cases, created by narrowing the controversy to its essential issues.

CONSTRUCTIVE SPEECH. The main speech in a debate for each speaker, in which all issues to be considered in the debate are presented.

CONTENTION. An argumentative statement that forms a main heading in the constructive outline and is supported by arguments and evidence.

COUNTERPLAN. In policy debates, a negative strategy that accepts the need but offers an alternative solution.

COUNTERWARRANT. In value-oriented debate, a negative strategy that argues for the acceptance of an alternative value structure from that called for by the resolution.

CRITICISM. Comments provided by a judge or teacher with the intent of explaining an evaluation and indicating areas in need of improvement.

CROSS-EXAMINATION. The process of asking questions of opposing speakers.

DEBATE. Formal oral controversy consisting of the systematic presentation of opposing arguments on a selected topic.

DELIVERY. The communication of ideas to an audience through verbal and nonverbal means.

EVIDENCE. Matters of fact or opinion offered as support or proof for assertions advanced.

EXAMPLE. A type of argument that asserts a generalization based on the qualities of a specific instance or instances.

FALLACY. Any defect in reasoning that destroys its validity.

FLOW SHEET. A method of taking notes during a debate that enables the debater or listener to keep track of the development of an argument throughout successive speeches. It represents the flow of argument in the debate.

FORENSICS. Speaking for judgment, often used to designate competitive interscholastic speech activities, such as debate. In this context, forensics is an educational activity primarily concerned with using an argumentative perspective in examining problems and communicating with people.

ISSUE. A conclusion that must be proved in order to establish that the proposition ought to be adopted; it appears in the debate as a key assertion.

JUDGE. The person who evaluates a debate.

LINCOLN-DOUGLAS DEBATE. Format in which one person confronts another in the tradition of the famous historical debates between Abraham Lincoln and Stephen Douglas.

NDT. National Debate Tournament; also, a shorthand term to designate policy proposition debate and the style of presentation associated with it.

NEED ISSUE. In policy-centered debate, an assertion by the affirmative side that there is need for a substantial change in the status quo.

NEGATIVE SIDE. The speaker or team that undertakes to prevent the affirmative side from securing acceptance of the debate proposition.

OBSERVATION. A preliminary remark that usually lays out a basic assumption or context prior to the presentation of contentions in a debate case.

OUTLINE. A carefully prepared structural pattern for a speech or case that clarifies the relationship of ideas in the message by placing information in a reasoned sequence and by indicating the coordinate and subordinate relationship of ideas.

PARLIAMENTARY DEBATE. A debate format that fosters communicative reasoning, often using extemporaneous topics and nomenclature adapted from parliamentary forms of government.

PRIMA FACIE CASE. A case that establishes such a high degree of probability that the proposition would be accepted unless the case is refuted; usually established in the first affirmative constructive speech.

PROOF. Support for an idea or argument that the speaker offers to create belief in an audience. In debate, it consists of evidence and reasoning that is offered to the audience.

PROPOSITION. A judgment expressed in a declarative

statement. In debate, it appears as an affirmative statement of the question to be resolved.

PROPOSITION OF POLICY. A proposition that a certain future action should be taken.

PROPOSITION OF VALUE. One of several types of propositions that do not call for a future action but make an evaluation or judgment.

QUOTATION. A noun referring to material that is being quoted.

QUOTE. A verb meaning to use words, sentences, or material from sources other than yourself; used by some as a slang abbreviation for the noun *quotation*.

REASONING. The process of drawing inferences and conclusions from available information or data; in debate, the process of inferring relationships between evidence and assertions.

REBUTTAL. The process of defending arguments against attack; in debate, an additional speech allowed each speaker following the constructive speeches in which a speaker may attack the opponents' arguments in addition to defense but may not introduce any new constructive arguments.

REFUTATION. The attempt to demonstrate the error or inadequacy of the opponents' case.

RESEARCH. The process of finding information and material to support ideas or arguments, most effective when conducted as the result of a carefully focused approach.

RESOLUTION. Used in the same way as *proposition*.

SIGN. A type of argument that asserts that the existence of fact A reliably indicates the existence of fact B.

STATUS QUO. Literally, "the state in which a thing is." In debate, it refers to the situation in existence as the debate begins.

STOCK ISSUES. The standard, or routine, issues that occur in almost every debate.

TOURNAMENT. The competitive gathering of speakers for various events, such as debate.

VALUES. General statements of principles on which one bases actions and beliefs.

WARRANT. The reasoning process by which we look at one bit of information (data) and decide what it means (claim).

JOHN M. ERICSON is the dean emeritus of the College of Liberal Arts at California Polytechnic State University, San Luis Obispo. He served as president of the Northern California Forensic Association (NCFA) and is a member of the forensics honor societies Pi Kappa Delta and Delta Sigma Rho. He founded the American Issues debate tournaments on value questions while he was the director of forensics at Stanford University.

JAMES J. MURPHY is a professor emeritus of rhetoric and communication and advisor to the Emil Mrak Forensic Union at the University of California, Davis. He was the founding president of the NCFA and has been a director of forensics at Stanford University and a faculty advisor to the Whig-Closophic forensics society at Princeton University.

RAYMOND BUD ZEUSCHNER is a professor of speech communication and has directed forensics at California Polytechnic State University; California State University, Northridge; and Los Angeles City College. He is a past president of the Cross Examination Debate Association, the NCFA, and the Pacific Southwest Collegiate Forensics Association and has served two terms as president of Phi Rho Pi, the National Community College Speech Association.